Bridging Finance in the UK

Bridging Finance in the UK

A Comprehensive Guide to Short-Term Property Lending

Cristiano Bellavitis, PhD

BEP

BUSINESS EXPERT PRESS

Leader in applied, concise business books

Bridging Finance in the UK:
A Comprehensive Guide to Short-Term Property Lending

Cover design by Cristiano Bellavitis and Charlene Kronstedt

Interior design by S4Carlisle Publishing Services, Chennai, India

First published in 2025 by
Business Expert Press, LLC
222 East 46th Street, New York, NY 10017
www.businessexpertpress.com

ISBN-13: 978-1-63742-882-5 (paperback)
ISBN-13: 978-1-63742-883-2 (e-book)

Finance and Financial Management Collection

First edition: 2025

10 9 8 7 6 5 4 3 2 1

EU SAFETY REPRESENTATIVE
Mare Nostrum Group B.V.
Mauritskade 21D
1091 GC Amsterdam
The Netherlands
gpsr@mare-nostrum.co.uk

Description

Unlock the Power of Bridging Finance for UK Property Investment

This practical and accessible book demystifies bridging finance—a vital tool for modern property investors. Drawing on real-world experience and expert insights, the book guides you through how short-term loans can fund flips, HMOs, title splits, and rental stabilizations. Whether you are an investor seeking to scale your portfolio or a borrower navigating fast-moving deals, this book offers strategic advice, clear explanations, and real case studies.

You'll learn how to assess costs, structure deals, work with lenders, and avoid common pitfalls. With insights from investors, brokers, and lenders across the UK, this is the go-to guide for mastering short-term property finance.

Who should read it?

Property investors, brokers, and finance professionals looking to leverage bridging loans effectively.

Why now?

With the UK market evolving rapidly, understanding bridging finance has never been more essential.

About the Authors

Prof. Cristiano Bellavitis is an associate professor of entrepreneurship and finance at the Stevens Institute of Technology, United States, where he focuses on entrepreneurial and digital finance. He serves as an associate editor for *Entrepreneurship Theory and Practice* and is a former co-editor of *Venture Capital: An International Journal of Entrepreneurial Finance*.

Prof. Bellavitis is also the founder of Integer Investments, a real estate investment and lending firm with a portfolio spanning London, New York, and Italy. Over more than a decade, Integer's real estate investments have generated a compounded ROE of 15.8 percent, and its lending arm stands among the fastest growing finance providers in the UK.

This multifaceted experience—combining rigorous research with real-world investing—allows Prof. Bellavitis to offer firsthand insights on bridging finance, short-term lending, and the broader property market. His goal is to help investors and industry professionals understand how bridging loans can unlock timely, profitable opportunities in a fast-paced and complex sector.

Luke Higgins is a property investor from Sunderland, England, whose real estate journey began in 2018. Growing up in a working-class family on a council estate, Luke initially viewed property investment as out of reach. However, after becoming an accidental landlord—renting out his personal home and moving back in with his parents—he discovered bridging finance and quickly scaled his operations. By 2024, Luke had assembled a multimillion-pound portfolio encompassing buy-to-lets, serviced accommodations, and HMOs (houses in multiple occupation) in his local region. His hands-on experience, combined with a keen understanding of short-term lending, has helped him thrive in the competitive UK property market.

Dean Parata is the founder and managing director of Parata Property, established in 2020 to meet the growing demand for HMO property sourcing and development in the UK. Drawing on his background as a professional rugby player, Dean applies a strong sense of teamwork and leadership to the property world, overseeing a team that delivers comprehensive, turnkey services for investors.

Parata Property specializes in HMO sourcing, project management, and refurbishment—particularly in the North West of England. Under Dean's guidance, the company has successfully completed over 70 projects, with a total transaction value surpassing £35 million and an average ROI of 18 percent. Dean's practical experience and strategic insights make him a trusted partner for both national and international clients looking to navigate the complexities of the UK real estate market.

Carlos Torres is a dual-qualified lawyer in England and Wales and in Brazil, with experience in real estate transactions, commercial law, and corporate support. He advises corporations, individuals, and financial institutions on property acquisitions, disposals, and refinances, including bridging finance transactions in the UK. His real estate experience further encompasses transactions in Brazil. In addition, Carlos assists clients with a wide range of business-to-business contractual matters, providing strategic legal support for commercial transactions.

Derek Walczak is the CEO and founder of W.P.D Property Investments Group Limited, located in Northwest England. Under Derek's leadership, W.P.D focuses on flipping residential properties and converting them into HMOs. Embracing bridging finance has allowed the company to scale rapidly and seize profitable opportunities in the fast-moving UK property market.

Contents

CHAPTER 1

Introduction to Bridging Finance in the UK Property Market

1.1 What Is Bridging Finance?

Bridging finance in the UK property market refers to short-term loans that provide quick funding to property investors, developers, or homeowners who need immediate access to capital. These loans are typically used to "bridge" a funding gap, often when investors need fast access to finance for a short period. Bridging loans are particularly popular in property projects like flipping, converting properties into HMOs (houses in multiple occupation), or developing new properties.

The primary attraction of bridging finance is its flexibility and speed. While traditional mortgages take time to arrange, bridging loans can be set up quickly, allowing investors to move forward with time-sensitive deals. Also, unlike banks, bridging lenders are willing to invest in properties that need substantial renovations. The short-term nature of these loans, typically between 4 and 12 months, and their higher interest rates make them ideal for investors who need financing for property purchases, refurbishments, or developments. Once the project is complete, the investor refinances with lower-cost, long-term finance, such as a mortgage, or sells the property to repay the bridging loan.

1.2 Historical Background and Growth of Bridging Finance in Property Investments

Bridging finance as a niche financial product has seen significant growth in the UK property sector over the past two decades. Initially, bridging loans were considered a last resort for borrowers who couldn't secure traditional financing. However, as the property market became more competitive, especially in urban areas, bridging finance emerged as a critical tool for investors needing quick access to capital.

The global financial crisis of 2008 played a significant role in the rise of bridging finance. As traditional banks tightened their lending criteria, property investors and developers faced challenges securing long-term financing. Specialist bridging lenders entered the market to fill this gap, offering faster approvals and greater flexibility than conventional banks. The main UK lenders in 2024 are Octopus Capital, Together Finance, and Integer Investments, among others. Today, the bridging finance industry is a multibillion-pound sector, with many lenders catering to property investors looking for fast, short-term financing.

The growing demand for bridging loans in the UK is closely linked to the increasing value of property, particularly in cities like London, Manchester, and Birmingham. Investors and developers need quick access to capital to secure properties before prices rise further. Bridging finance provides the flexibility they need to act quickly, making it an indispensable tool for property investment.

1.3 The Popularity of Bridging Loans in the UK Property Market

The demand for bridging finance has surged in the UK, driven by the flexibility and speed that property investors need in a competitive market. According to the EY UK Bridging Market Survey 2024, the total loan book size of respondents reached approximately £5.9 billion, a clear indication of the sector's growth. The ability to access short-term loans quickly makes bridging finance particularly appealing to property investors involved in flipping, conversions, and developments (Ernst & Young 2024).

One significant driver of demand is for refurbishment purposes, with 33 percent of respondents citing it as the primary reason for obtaining bridging loans. This trend has been consistent across previous years, as investors seek to add value to properties quickly before selling or refinancing. Another growing factor is auction purchases or mortgage delays. In 2024, 19 percent of respondents indicated that they used bridging finance to purchase at auction and 16 percent due to delays in securing traditional mortgages. This reflects the ongoing slowdown in the mortgage market and the increased need for short-term financing solutions (Ernst & Young 2024).

The average loan-to-value (LTV) ratios for bridging loans have remained conservative. The EY survey reported that 64 percent of respondents maintained LTVs between 60 percent and 70 percent, highlighting a cautious approach amid concerns over property price fluctuations. However, higher LTVs exist. For example, at Integer Investments, for repeated borrowers with good credit history and experience, it reached 90 percent, although 80 to 85 percent is usually the upper limit. According to the EY survey, in 2024 only 5 percent of lenders offer above 80 percent LTV. Moreover, 46 percent of lenders noted that average loan terms range between 9 and 12 months, which aligns with the short-term nature of these loans. This is particularly beneficial for property investors who only need financing for a few months before refinancing with a lower-cost mortgage once their project is complete (Ernst & Young 2024).

In terms of interest rates, the EY survey reports the following distribution:

- Fifty-six percent of lenders charge between 1 and 1.25 percent.
- Thirty-eight percent charge between 0.75 and 1 percent.
- Six percent charge above 1.25 percent or below 0.75 percent.

However, it is important to note that some lenders offer a teaser interest rate that is valid only for a few months (generally 1 to 4), and then the interest grows significantly. For example, it could be 0.6 percent for 3 months, and then 1.5 percent for the remainder of the loan. This example, in 12 months, equals an overall rate of 1.275 percent. In addition, as we will discuss later, lenders charge various fees that can significantly alter the cost of the loan.

According to the EY respondents, higher interest rates (30 percent) and macroeconomic uncertainty (18 percent) remain the top challenges noted by the most participants in the survey in 2024. An increase in challenges arising from higher interest rates is expected, given the knock-on impact on lender margins, profitability, levels of defaults, and loan performance if not carefully managed. Operationally, 95 percent of lenders declared that protracted legal processes are a challenge and an obstacle to their business. This is by far the main challenge experienced by lenders.

Despite these challenges, the outlook for the UK bridging market remains optimistic. According to the EY survey, 67 percent of respondents expect growth in annual originations. Market participants' views of macroeconomic uncertainty have also reduced since the 2023 survey. However, the sector remains vigilant in a higher interest rate environment, and the path of interest rates, loan performance, and foreclosure activity were all areas of increased focus for the survey participants in 2024. This is largely because bridging lenders are well positioned to fill gaps in the market left by stricter mortgage lending (Ernst & Young 2024).

1.4 Why Bridging Finance Appeals to UK Property Investors

Bridging loans offer several advantages to UK property investors, particularly those involved in flipping properties, refurbishments, or new developments:

- **Speed**: Bridging loans can be arranged in days, making them ideal for time-sensitive transactions such as auction purchases or property renovations. Traditional mortgages, by contrast, can take weeks or months to arrange. It is important to note that the transaction is usually slowed down by conveyancers when buying a property. To clarify, a bridging lender, once all documents and surveys are available, should be able to disburse funds in 24 hours. However, obtaining Land Registry searches and satisfying the solicitors' due diligence can take much longer, slowing down the entire process. Usually, purchasing transactions takes about 2 months. One way to streamline the legal process is to work with a bridging lender who offers dual representation. In this case, there will be two solicitors (the buyer's and seller's) and the buyer's solicitor will also represent the lender. If this solution is chosen, it is important to make sure that there are no conflicts of interest.
- **Short-Term Financing**: Property investors typically need financing for short periods, especially when flipping properties

or undertaking quick developments. Bridging loans are designed for short-term use, with loan terms typically ranging from 4 to 12 months. Some lenders charge a minimum period of interest. For example, Integer Investments charges a minimum of 4 months of interest. It is also important to note that most bridging lenders expect the loan to be fully repaid within 12 months (or the agreed period). If this is not possible, extension fees are charged and usually they represent 1 to 5 percent of the total loan, adding significant costs to the project.

- **Refinancing for Lower-Cost Finance**: Once a project is complete, investors often refinance with a conventional mortgage, which offers lower interest rates, making bridging finance a cost-effective interim solution. For example, an investor might use a bridging loan to purchase and renovate a property, then refinance with a longer-term mortgage once the property's value has increased (due to the renovation improvements). At the time of writing, the beginning of 2025, a bridging loan comes with an interest of about 1 percent a month, as opposed to about 5 percent a year for a buy-to-let (BTL) mortgage with a 65 to 70 percent LTV (0.42 percent a month).
- **Flexible Terms**: Bridging finance offers flexible repayment options, such as rolling up interest payments until the loan is repaid, which suits investors who may not have immediate cash flow during a project.

Bridging finance has proven to be particularly effective for property investors who understand the importance of speed and flexibility in the real estate market. However, investors must ensure they have a clear exit strategy, such as refinancing or selling the property, to avoid the higher costs of extending the loan beyond its original term.

Conclusion: The Role of Bridging Finance in the UK Property Market

In the fast-paced UK property market, bridging finance plays a critical role in enabling investors to seize opportunities quickly. Whether it's flipping properties, building new developments, or converting properties into HMOs, bridging loans provide the short-term funding necessary to make these projects viable. The ability to refinance with lower-cost conventional finance upon project completion makes bridging finance a crucial tool for investors who need flexibility without long-term commitments.

As we move forward in this book, we'll explore the different types of bridging loans available to property investors, how to navigate the legal and regulatory framework, and advanced strategies for maximizing returns using bridging finance.

Case Study: Transforming a Council House into a Profitable Investment (By Luke Higgins)

The Investment Opportunity

In April 2024, Luke identified a promising investment opportunity: a two-bedroom, semidetached, ex–local authority house located in Sunderland. The property was situated in a high-demand rental area, particularly appealing to families due to its proximity to schools, transport links, and significant local employers like the nearby car manufacturing facilities that had recently received billions in investment from Nissan (source: www.gov.uk/government/news/issan-triples-investment-in-electric-vehicle-production-in-the-uk).

The house was in poor condition, featuring dated amenities and requiring a full modernization. However, Luke recognized its potential immediately. Having grown up in the same council estate, he was acutely aware of the local demand for quality rental properties. Moreover, he saw an opportunity to increase the property's value and rental appeal by converting it from a two-bedroom to a three-bedroom home through strategic renovations.

Investment Strategy

Luke's overarching strategy was to purchase the property at an attractive price, undertake renovations to modernize and improve it, and then rent it out to meet the high local demand. By adding an extra bedroom and enhancing the property's features, he aimed to significantly increase both its gross development value (GDV) and rental income. The end goal was to refinance the property onto a traditional mortgage, thereby releasing the capital invested and allowing him to repeat the process with additional properties.

The Role of Bridging Finance in the Project

Necessity of Bridging Finance

The property was being sold at auction with terms requiring completion within 56 days. This tight deadline made traditional financing options unfeasible due to their longer approval and processing times. Having previously worked with Integer Investments, a specialist bridging finance lender, Luke knew that bridging finance could provide the quick, flexible funding solution he needed.

Overcoming Challenges with Bridging Finance:

- **Speed of Purchase:** Bridging finance enabled Luke to secure the necessary funds swiftly, ensuring he met the auction's completion deadline.
- **Property Condition:** Traditional lenders often hesitate to finance properties in poor condition. The bridging loan did not impose such constraints, allowing Luke to purchase a property that required significant renovation.
- **Capital Allocation:** By financing a substantial portion of the purchase and refurbishment costs through the bridging loan, Luke could conserve his own capital for contingencies and other investment opportunities.

Facilitation of the Investment Strategy:
Using bridging finance, Luke was able to:

- **Secure the Property Quickly:** Receive a same-day lending offer and begin the conveyancing process immediately.

- **Fund Renovations:** Cover a portion of the refurbishment costs, essential for converting the property into a three-bedroom home and increasing its market value.
- **Implement Exit Strategy:** Plan to refinance onto a traditional mortgage after renovations, repaying the bridging loan and freeing up capital for future investments.

Detailed Financial Breakdown

Purchase Details:
- **Purchase Price:** £68,000
- **Initial Valuation:** The property's value was aligned with the purchase price due to its poor condition.
- **Negotiation:** Luke leveraged his knowledge of the area and the property's potential to confidently bid at auction, securing the property at a favorable price.

Bridging Loan Details:
- **Loan Amount:** £71,033
  - This amount covered a portion of the purchase price (£62,900) and a portion of the refurbishment costs (£8,133).
- **Loan-to-Value (LTV) Ratio:** Approximately 85 percent of the purchase price and renovations.
- **Lender Selection:** Integer Investments was chosen for their efficiency, flexibility, and previous positive experience.
- **Interest Rate:** 1 percent per month
- **Fees and Costs:**
  - **Arrangement Fee:** 2.5 percent of the loan amount (£1,775.83)
  - **Legal Fees:** £1,634
  - **Valuation Fee:** Around £500
- **Loan Term:** 12 months
- **Interest Payment Structure:** Monthly payments
- **Special Terms:** Quick approval process and flexibility in funding renovations. A discount was provided as the borrower had extensive experience with similar projects, a good credit score, and had worked with the lender before.

Refurbishment Costs:

- **Total Refurbishment Costs:** £14,600
  - **Kitchen and Bathroom Upgrades:** £4,000
  - **Décor and Flooring:** £4,000
  - **Heating System (New Central Heating):** £2,000
  - **Window Replacement (Double Glazing):** £1,600
  - **Structural Modifications (Removing Walls, Subdividing Bedroom):** £3,000

Additional Costs:

- **Stamp Duty Land Tax (SDLT):** As the property was under £125,000, SDLT was likely minimal or exempt for a first-time buyer, but as an additional property, a 3 percent surcharge may apply (£68,000 × 3 percent = £2,040).
- **Insurance:** £200
- **Holding Costs:** Utilities and council tax during renovation (estimated at £200 for two months).
- **Other costs:** £1,834
- **Total Additional Costs:** Approximately £4,074

Total Investment:

- **Total Costs:** Purchase Price (£68,000) + Refurbishment (£14,600) + Additional Costs (£4,074) = £86,674
- **Total Bridging Loan Repayment:** Principal (£71,033) + Interest (1 percent × 12 months × £71,033 = £8,524) + Fees (£1,775.83 arrangement fee + £1,634 legal fees + £500 valuation fee) = £83,466.83
- **Investor's Capital Contribution:** Total Costs (£86,674) − Bridging Loan (£71,033) = £15,641

The Renovation Process

Steps Taken:

1. **Structural Modifications:**
   - **Removal of Non–Load Bearing Walls:** Created an open-plan living and dining area, enhancing the property's appeal.

- ○ **Subdivision of Front Bedroom:** Converted the property from a two-bedroom to a three-bedroom home, increasing rental demand and property value.

2. **Upgrades and Installations:**
   - ○ **New Central Heating System:** Improved energy efficiency, reducing utility costs for tenants.
   - ○ **Window Replacement:** Upgraded from single-glazed to double-glazed windows, enhancing insulation and security.
   - ○ **Kitchen Installation:** Fitted a modern kitchen with integrated oven and hob, increasing the property's marketability.
   - ○ **Bathroom Renovation:** Transformed the outdated wet room into a modern bathroom with a bathtub, overhead shower, new wash basin, and toilet.

3. **Cosmetic Enhancements:**
   - ○ **Décor and Flooring:** Updated interior decor with fresh paint and new flooring throughout, providing a contemporary look.

Challenges Encountered:
- **Time Constraints:** Despite the ambitious renovation plan, the project was completed within two months due to efficient project management and coordination with contractors.
- **Budget Management:** Careful planning ensured the project stayed within budget, avoiding unexpected cost overruns.

Project Management:
- **Contractor Coordination:** Luke managed a team of trusted local contractors, ensuring work was completed to a high standard and on schedule.
- **Quality Assurance:** Regular site visits and inspections were conducted to maintain quality control.
- **Compliance:** The renovations met all local building regulations and safety standards, including the Housing Health and Safety Rating System (HHSRS).

Exit Strategy and Outcome

Execution of Exit Strategy:

- **Refinancing:** Upon completion of the renovations and securing a tenant, Luke refinanced the property onto a traditional BTL mortgage.
- **Valuation:** The property's post-refurbishment valuation was £125,000, reflecting the added value from the renovations and conversion to a three-bedroom home.
- **Mortgage Details:**
  - **Loan Amount:** Typically, buy-to-let lenders offer up to 75 percent LTV, equating to £93,750.
  - **Repayment of Bridging Loan:** The funds from the mortgage were used to repay the bridging loan of £83,466.83 (including interests).
  - **Capital Released:** The mortgage covered the bridging loan repayment, with surplus funds available for future investments.

Financial Results:

- **Rental Income:** Achieved a rental agreement at £750 per calendar month.
- **Annual Rental Income:** £9,000
- **Mortgage Payments:** Assuming an interest rate of 5 percent on £93,750, the annual mortgage interest would be approximately £4,688.
- **Net Annual Income:** Rental Income (£9,000) − Mortgage Interest (£4,688) = £4,312
- **Return on Investment (ROI):**
  - **Investor's Capital Remaining in Deal:** Total Investment (£86,674) − Mortgage (£93,750) = −£7,076 (indicating that Luke was able to pull out more capital than he invested)
  - **Total Profit from Refinancing:** Capital Released (£7,076) + Net Annual Income (£4,312) = £11,388
- **Project Duration:** 6 months from purchase to refinancing.

Accolades and Recognition:

- **Council Accreditation:** Luke received an accreditation from the local council, recognizing the property as being "in an excellent condition internally and externally" and fully compliant with HHSRS standards.
- **Media Feature:** The property and Luke's investment journey were featured on the popular UK television show "Homes Under the Hammer," highlighting the success of the project.

Lessons Learned and Advice

Reflections on the Project:

- **Success Factors:**
  - **Local Knowledge:** Luke's familiarity with the area and understanding of market demand were crucial in identifying the property's potential.
  - **Efficient Use of Bridging Finance:** Quick access to funds allowed him to secure the property and complete renovations within a tight time frame.
  - **Value Addition:** Strategic renovations significantly increased the property's value and rental appeal.
- **Challenges Overcome:**
  - **Time Pressure:** Managing the auction purchase timeline and renovation schedule required meticulous planning.
  - **Budget Adherence:** Keeping the project within budget was essential to ensure profitability.

Advice for Other Investors:

- **Utilize Bridging Finance Wisely:** Bridging loans are powerful tools for rapid acquisitions, especially in auction scenarios, but require careful planning and clear exit strategies.
- **Conduct Thorough Due Diligence:** Understand the local market, property condition, and potential renovation costs before investing.

- **Have Multiple Exit Strategies:** Luke emphasizes the importance of having at least two clear exit strategies to repay the bridging loan, such as refinancing or selling the property.
- **Work with Trusted Partners:** Building relationships with reliable lenders, contractors, and legal professionals can streamline the investment process.
- **Add Value Strategically:** Look for opportunities to enhance properties in ways that significantly increase value, such as adding bedrooms or modern amenities.

Conclusion

Impact of Bridging Finance on Project Success:
Bridging finance was instrumental in the success of Luke's investment. It provided the necessary speed and flexibility to secure the auction property and fund essential renovations. By leveraging this financing method, Luke was able to transform a dilapidated house into a modern, energy-efficient home, significantly increasing its value and rental income potential.

Benefits of Bridging Finance for Similar Projects:
- **Quick Acquisition:** Ideal for auction purchases or properties requiring immediate action.
- **Flexibility:** Accommodates properties that may not qualify for traditional financing due to condition.
- **Capital Efficiency:** Enables investors to undertake projects without tying up large amounts of personal capital.

Future Use of Bridging Finance:
Luke intends to continue using bridging finance for future projects, recognizing it as a key component in scaling his property portfolio. He advocates for its use among investors who, like himself, may not have substantial personal wealth but have the knowledge and skills to identify and enhance valuable property investments.

By sharing his experience, Luke Higgins provides a practical example of how bridging finance can be effectively utilized in property investment, particularly for auction purchases and value-adding renovations. His story illustrates the importance of strategic planning, local market understanding, and the ability to act swiftly when opportunities arise.

References

Ernst & Young. *UK Bridging Market Survey 2024*. 2024. https://www.ey.com /en_uk/real-estate-hospitality-construction/uk-bridging-market-survey-2024

CHAPTER 2

Types of Bridging Loans for UK Property Investors

Bridging loans come in several varieties, each tailored to different circumstances and needs within the UK property market. For investors, it's essential to understand the key distinctions between these types, as the right choice of loan can significantly impact the success of a property investment.

2.1 Closed Versus Open Bridging Loans

Closed bridging loans are structured with a definitive exit strategy and a fixed repayment date. These are ideal for investors who have a clear plan for repaying the loan, such as waiting for a property sale or finalizing a long-term mortgage. Typically, a borrower using a closed loan has already exchanged contracts on a property and is just waiting for completion. This predictability lowers the lender's risk, which often results in slightly better terms for the borrower.

For example, at Integer Investments, closed bridging loans are offered to investors who need a short-term funding solution while working on the renovation of a property or waiting for conventional mortgage approval. Because there's a defined timeline (usually 4 to 12 months), the terms can be more favorable than open bridging loans, with lower interest rates or fees.

Open bridging loans, on the other hand, do not have a set repayment date, although they are typically expected to be repaid within 12 months. Open loans are more flexible but come with higher interest rates due to the increased risk for the lender. These loans are usually taken out by investors who may not have a confirmed exit strategy, such as those purchasing properties at auction without a buyer or refinancing plan lined up. For instance, investors planning extensive renovations might use an open loan while searching for a buyer or arranging longer-term finance post-completion.

2.2 First- and Second-Charge Bridging Loans

Bridging loans are categorized by their "charge" on the property, which refers to the priority of repayment in the event of a default.

First-charge bridging loans are secured against a property that is not already mortgaged, or where the bridging lender takes priority over any existing lender. The lender with the first charge has the first right to the proceeds from the sale of the property if the borrower defaults. These loans generally offer lower interest rates because the lender has a stronger claim on the collateral. These loans can achieve up to 90 percent loan to value (LTV). This means that if the property is worth £100,000, the borrower can raise up to £90,000.

First-charge loans are often used by property investors purchasing properties outright or who are willing to pay off existing mortgages to secure the first charge. These loans are ideal for investors with a clear exit strategy and sufficient equity in the property.

Second-charge bridging loans, by contrast, are secured against properties that already have a mortgage. The second-charge lender only has the right to repayment once the first-charge lender has been paid in full. Because of this subordinate position, second-charge loans come with higher interest rates and stricter terms. They are useful for investors who need to raise capital quickly but do not want to refinance or pay off their existing mortgage.

Second-charge loans are often used for renovation projects or smaller capital needs where the investor doesn't want to disrupt their existing mortgage arrangements. For instance, an investor might take out a second-charge loan to finance the conversion of a property into an HMO (house in multiple occupation), without affecting their first mortgage. These loans usually can achieve up to 70 percent LTV, combined between first and second charge. For example, if the house is worth £100,000, and the first mortgage has an outstanding balance of £50,000, the borrower can only raise an additional £20,000. Considering the fees and legal costs involved, this strategy is not always convenient. In this case, for example, assuming £2,000 in legal fees, 2 percent in acceptance fee and a 1.2 percent a month interest, the cost would be prohibitive. Assuming a 6-month bridge:

- £2,000 in legals
- £400 in acceptance fee
- £240/month in interest, £1,440 for 6 months
  - Total: £3,840

Hence, even without an exit fee, the total interest is £3,840, representing 19.2 percent for just 6 months of capital. Hence, this strategy only works when there is plenty of equity in the property so that the total loan value can be higher. Further, not all banks and lenders agree to adding a second charge, or the conversion of a property. Therefore, borrowers need to consult with the first-charge lender before trying to raise capital through a second charge. In some cases, refinancing the entire mortgage, ideally with a conventional mortgage, can be more convenient than adding a second-charge lender.

2.3 Regulated Versus Unregulated Bridging Loans

Regulated bridging loans are governed by the Financial Conduct Authority (FCA) and typically involve residential properties where the borrower or their immediate family intends to live in the property. These loans must comply with stringent regulations designed to protect consumers, including affordability assessments and clear communication of loan terms. As a result, regulated bridging loans are more common among homeowners who need short-term funding but plan to refinance or sell the property.

For property investors, regulated loans are less commonly used, as most bridging loans are taken out for investment properties rather than personal residences. However, in some cases, an investor might seek a regulated bridging loan if they plan to purchase a residential property they intend to live in temporarily while refurbishing another.

Unregulated bridging loans, on the other hand, are more commonly used in property investments, as they involve properties that will not serve as the borrower's primary residence. These loans do not fall under the FCA's oversight, allowing for more flexibility in terms of the loan structure, terms, and repayment options. Because they are geared toward experienced investors, unregulated loans often come with fewer restrictions and quicker approvals. However, the trade-off is that borrowers have less protection if issues arise. Unregulated bridging loans offered to property investors typically involve properties intended for flipping, conversions, or development.

Conclusion: Choosing the Right Type of Bridging Loan

Selecting the right type of bridging loan is crucial for UK property investors. The decision between closed and open loans depends largely on the investor's exit strategy and the certainty of their financing plans. First- and second-charge loans offer different levels of flexibility and risk, while regulated versus unregulated loans cater to different types of borrowers and properties.

By understanding these distinctions, property investors can ensure that they choose the most suitable financing option for their needs, whether they're looking to flip properties, complete renovations, or bridge a temporary gap in funding. At Integer Investments, we work closely with investors to determine the best loan structure for their specific projects, offering flexible terms to help maximize returns.

In the next chapter, we'll explore the key uses of bridging finance in property investments, from buying at auction to refinancing after property improvements.

CHAPTER 3

Key Uses of Bridging Finance in Property Investments

Bridging finance is a highly flexible tool that can be applied in several property investment scenarios. The fast access to capital and short-term nature of bridging loans makes them particularly useful for investors looking to capitalize on time-sensitive opportunities, such as property auctions, refurbishments, and conversions. In this chapter, we'll explore some of the most common and strategic uses of bridging finance in the UK property market.

3.1 Buying Property at Auction

One of the most common uses of bridging finance in property investment is purchasing properties at auction. Auctions are fast-paced environments, and buyers typically need to complete the transaction within 28 days of winning a bid. This tight time frame often makes it impossible to secure a traditional mortgage, which can take several weeks or even months to arrange.

In these cases, investors turn to bridging loans as a solution. A bridging loan provides the necessary funds to complete the purchase within the auction's time frame, allowing investors to secure the property. After the property is purchased, the investor can either sell it quickly for a profit or refinance with a traditional mortgage to repay the bridging loan.

Another important factor for investors buying properties at auctions is the fact that, generally, auction properties are not in great condition, making them an unlikely candidate for traditional bank financing.

Bridging allows investors to secure the property, renovate it, and make it habitable and then refinance it with lower cost financing.

For example, Integer Investments regularly works with clients who purchase properties at auction. By providing fast, flexible loans, we enable investors to secure properties without worrying about lengthy approval processes. Once all documentation is ready, which at auction is provided in a pack, the loan approval can take as little as a few hours. Once the auction purchase is complete, the investor can refurbish or resell the property to exit the loan.

Example: Auction Purchase and Quick Resale

Property Purchase and Financing:
- **Purchase Price:** £300,000
- **Renovation Costs:** £20,000
- **Total Loan (80 percent LTV on purchase and renovation):** £240,000 (purchase) + £16,000 (renovation) = **£256,000**
- **Investor's Contribution (deposit + renovation):** £60,000 (deposit) + £4,000 (renovation) = **£64,000**

Additional Costs:
- **Product Fee:** 1.5 percent of £256,000 = **£3,840**
- **Exit Fee:** 1 percent of £256,000 = **£2,560**
- **Interest:** 0.95 percent per month for 6 months on £256,000 = **£14,592**
- **Legal Fees:** £2,000
- **Valuation Costs:** £500
- **Other Closing Costs:** £500

Total Investor Capital:
- **Investor's Contribution:** £64,000
- **All Additional Costs:** £3,840 + £2,560 + £14,592 + £2,000 + £500 + £500 = **£23,992**
- **Total Capital Deployed:** £64,000 + £23,992 = **£87,992**

Sale Price:
- **Sold for**: £375,000

Profit Calculation:
- **Profit**: £375,000 − (£256,000 loan repayment + £87,992 total costs) = £375,000 − £343,992 = **£31,008**

Raw ROI:
- **ROI**: (£30,008 ÷ £87,992) × 100 = **35.2 percent**

Annualized ROI:
Since the project took 6 months, the **annualized** ROI is:

- **35.2 percent ÷ 0.5 = 70.5 percent%**

This project is profitable both in terms of ROI but also because it was finished in 6 months rather than 12. The risk also seems manageable since the renovation is not too extensive.

3.2 Property Flipping and Renovations

Another common application of bridging finance is property flipping— purchasing a property, renovating it, and reselling it for profit within a short time frame. Investors often choose bridging loans for these projects because they typically only need financing for a few months.

When selecting a lender, it's crucial to find one that offers the right structure. Some lenders will only fund the purchase, while others are willing to finance renovations as well. In the latter scenario, funds are released in stages—for example, an initial tranche might cover the property purchase (e.g., £80,000), followed by three disbursements of £20,000 each as renovation milestones are met. Since lenders usually release capital only once these milestones are completed, it's important to have a capital buffer on hand to cover interim expenses.

Because the goal is a quick profit through resale, short-term solutions like bridging loans are ideal. Once the property sells, the proceeds repay the loan, eliminating the need for a longer-term mortgage that doesn't suit a brief project timeline.

At Integer Investments, many of our clients successfully flip properties using bridging finance. In one recent example, we provided a 6-month loan to purchase and refurbish a three-bedroom house in Manchester. The loan covered 85 percent of the purchase price (£80,750) plus three renovation disbursements totaling £36,465. After completing the refurb, the investor sold the property for a substantial profit, repaid the loan on schedule, and wrapped up the entire transaction in under seven months.

Example: Flipping a Residential Property

Property Purchase and Financing:
- **Purchase Price**: £200,000
- **Renovation Costs**: £40,000
- **Total Loan (75 percent** LTV **on purchase and renovation)**: £150,000 (purchase) + £30,000 (renovation) = **£180,000**
- **Investor's Contribution (deposit + renovation)**: £50,000 (deposit) + £10,000 (renovation) = **£60,000**

Additional Costs:
- **Product Fee**: 1.5 percent of £180,000 = **£2,700**
- **Exit Fee**: 1 percent of £180,000 = **£1,800**
- **Interest**: 1 percent per month for 12 months on £180,000 = **£21,600**
- **Legal Fees**: £2,000
- **Valuation Costs**: £500
- **Other Closing Costs**: £500

Total Investor Capital:
- **Investor's Contribution**: £60,000
- **All Additional Costs**: £2,700 + £1,800 + £21,600 + £2,000 + £500 + £500 = **£29,100**
- **Total Capital Deployed**: £60,000 + £29,100 = **£89,100**

Sale Price:
- **Sold for**: £275,000

Profit Calculation:
- **Profit**: £275,000 − (£180,000 loan repayment + £89,100 total costs) = £275,000 − £269,100 = **£5,900**

Raw ROI:
- **ROI**: (£5,900 ÷ £89,100) × 100 = **6.62 percent**

Annualized ROI:
Since the project took 12 months, the **annualized** ROI remains **6.62 percent**. In this case, the investor made a profit, but it is not great, especially because this example does not take into account selling costs that would probably wipe out the £5,900 in estimated profits. It is important to run your numbers in advance since not every property deal can remunerate your capital.

Case Study: Bridging Finance for a Six-Bedroom HMO Conversion (By Dean Parata)

Introduction

This case study examines the conversion of a three-bedroom terraced property into a six-bedroom, all en suite HMO (house in multiple occupation). The property was sourced through an online auction, allowing us to secure it via a pre-auction offer, thus avoiding competitive bidding.

A significant feature of the property was its unused double extension, which contributed three additional en suite bedrooms to the final design. With planning permission already in place, we reconfigured the interior layout to maximize rental capacity. Our strategy involved gutting the property and reconfiguring it with the help of an architect to meet HMO regulations. Room sizes were designed to meet the 6.5 m² minimum requirement, with en-suite rooms measuring 2.5 m², and communal spaces ranging from 20 m² to 35 m², in compliance with local council standards. The double extension provided an additional 15 m² on both levels, allowing us to create the three extra rooms while redesigning the existing space to house six en suite bedrooms. The floor plan here, prepared by AJM Architectural Services, outlines the changes implemented.

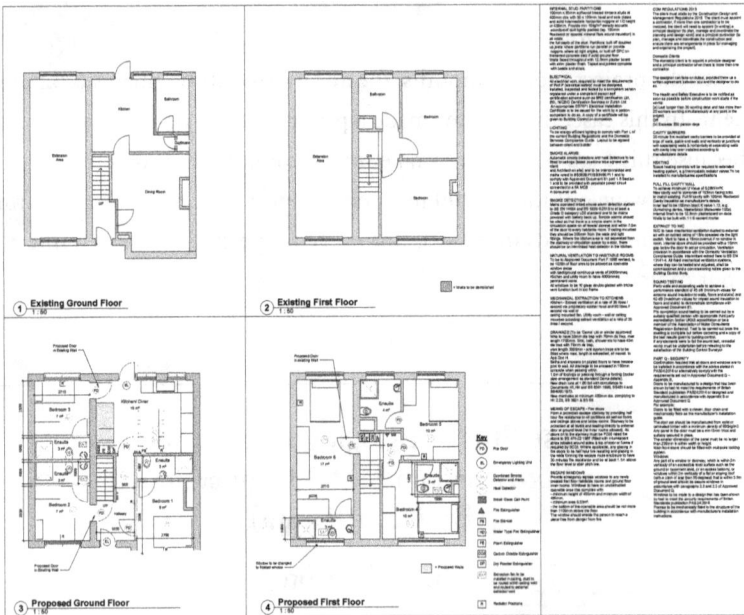

Renovation Details

The renovation of this property was extensive, involving five main phases:

1. **Demolition and Structural Adjustments**:
   - Removal of chimneys, reconfiguration of walls, and conversion of reception spaces to create en-suite bedrooms.
   - Stripping the house back to brick, applying damp treatments, and ensuring structural integrity for the extension.

2. **Reconfiguration and First Fixes**:
   - Installation of new electrical, plumbing, and heating systems, including a 30 kW boiler and thermostat.
   - Full fire safety upgrades with FD30 fire doors, interlinked alarms, and emergency lighting.
3. **Second Fixes and Finishes**:
   - Installation of a new kitchen, fire doors, skirting boards, architraves, and flooring.
   - En suite installations, furniture fitting, and redecoration.
4. **Final Checks and Compliance**:
   - Completion of snagging, deep cleaning, and certification of all works (EPC [engineering, procurement, and construction] and FRA [fire risk assessment]).
   - External work included roof repairs, gutter replacement, and landscaping the gardens.

The entire renovation was quoted at £90,000, including VAT, and was projected to take 22 weeks. The payment structure included a 20 percent upfront deposit (£18,000), with biweekly payments of £6,545.45 each over 11 instalments. Payments were required within 3 days of invoice issuance, and video updates were provided throughout the project.

Experience with Bridging Finance

Bridging finance was used to fund the acquisition and refurbishment of the property. We opted for a 75 percent LTV loan, which covered a significant portion of the property's purchase price, requiring a deposit of £30,000. The lender charged 2 percent in fees, and the broker 1 percent. The interest rate charged was 1 percent a month, and there were associated costs such as valuation that cost £1,850.

The process of managing the paperwork, proof of serviceability, and document certification was time-consuming. Additionally, the high interest rates associated with bridging loans meant that project delays would have led to increased costs. To avoid this, we worked closely with our build team and broker to ensure that the refurbishment was completed swiftly and that refinancing occurred promptly.

Detailed Financial Breakdown

Here are the detailed financial figures for this project using the 75 percent LTV strategy:

- **Purchase Price**: £120,000
- **Refurbishment Costs**: £90,000
- **Additional Project Costs**:
  - ○ Bridging/Refinance Fees: £7,250
  - ○ Solicitor Fees and Searches: £4,427
  - ○ Pre-auction Due Diligence: £6,900
  - ○ Reports, Planning, and Licensing: £1,203 (architectural drawings), £1,742 (HMO licensing), £725 (homebuyer's report)
  - ○ Utilities, Council Tax, and Insurance: £1,062
  - ○ Furniture, White Goods, and Blinds: £7,500
  - ○ **Total Cash Required for Project Conversion**: £150,809

Upon completion, the property was refinanced with a GDV (gross development value) of £250,000. The bridging and remortgage fees totaled £5,625, and after recycling 75 percent of the GDV, the capital left in the deal was £61,634.

Rental Income and Profitability

- **Anticipated Monthly Rent**: £3,300
- **Annual Rent**: £39,600
- **Mortgage Interest Payments (6.75 percent)**: £12,656 annually (interest-only mortgage)
- **Annual Running Costs**:
  - ○ Utilities, Council Tax, Broadband, Building Insurance, etc.: £6,493
  - ○ Management Fee (13 percent): £5,148
  - ○ Voids & Maintenance (10 percent): £3,960
- **Monthly Profit**: £1,374
- **Annual Profit**: £16,491
- Return on Investment (ROI): 26.76 percent

Conclusion

Bridging finance allowed us to transform this three-bedroom property into a six-bedroom HMO, making the project feasible despite initial capital constraints. The success of the project relied on efficient project management, timely refinancing, and completing the refurbishment within the estimated time frame to avoid excessive interest charges.

This project demonstrates the potential of bridging finance as a tool for unlocking property investments, particularly when well planned and executed.

3.3 Refinancing and Development Projects

In addition to flipping and renovations, bridging loans are frequently used by developers to cover short-term funding gaps in larger projects. For example, a developer might need to purchase land or secure planning permission before starting construction. In these cases, bridging finance can provide the necessary capital until a long-term development loan or mortgage is secured.

Bridging loans are also used to refinance existing loans on development projects. Developers might use a bridging loan to pay off an existing loan that is about to expire, giving them more time to secure a more favorable refinancing deal. This flexibility ensures that projects can continue without interruption while longer-term financing is arranged.

However, not all lenders are willing to fund ground-up developments due to the heightened risks. These projects involve building a property from scratch, which requires greater capital, specialized expertise, and a longer timescale than a standard refurbishment. Developers must also navigate potential delays in construction, unexpected site conditions, or shifting regulations. Consequently, lenders who do finance ground-up construction tend to scrutinize the developer's track record, project management skills, and contingency plans more rigorously. Having a robust skill set—including deep knowledge of planning permissions, budgets, and contractor oversight—can make the difference in securing a bridging loan for a ground-up project, as it reassures the lender that the development will reach completion on time and on budget.

3.4 Converting Properties to HMOs

Converting properties into houses in multiple occupation (HMOs) is another common use of bridging finance. Houses in multiple occupation are properties rented out to multiple tenants, typically providing higher rental yields compared to traditional buy-to-let (BTL) properties. Investors often purchase properties with the intention of converting them into HMOs to maximize rental income.

The conversion process can be expensive, requiring substantial renovations to meet HMO standards. Bridging loans provide the capital needed to complete the conversion. Once the conversion is finished and tenants are secured, the investor can refinance the property with a traditional BTL mortgage (not all BTL mortgages are suitable for HMO housing) or sell the property at a higher value.

At Integer Investments, we frequently work with investors who are converting properties into HMOs. One investor used a bridging loan to purchase a two-bedroom house and convert it into an HMO, adding one bathroom and three additional bedrooms. After the conversion was complete, the investor refinanced the property with a traditional mortgage and now enjoys higher rental yields and significant equity in the property.

Case study: HMO Conversion

Scenario Overview

An investor purchases a two-bedroom residential property for **£100,000** and plans to convert it into a six-bedroom HMO. The property will be rented out under a social housing scheme, where the housing provider covers most operational costs. Each room is rented for **£400** per month, providing a stable income stream with minimal expenses.

Property Acquisition and Conversion Plan

- **Purchase Price:** £100,000
- **Renovation Costs:** £80,000
  - **Breakdown of Renovation Costs:**
    - Converting existing space to create six bedrooms
    - Upgrading facilities to meet HMO and social housing standards
    - Installing safety features (fire doors, alarms)
    - Compliance with all relevant regulations
- Total Project Cost: £180,000 (£100,000 + £80,000)

Financing Structure

The investor uses bridging finance to fund 75 percent of the project cost and plans to sell the property after 10 months.

- Loan-to-Value (LTV): 75 percent of total project cost
- Bridging Loan Amount: 75 percent × £180,000 = £135,000
- Investor's Cash Contribution: 25 percent × £180,000 = £45,000
- Bridging Loan Details:
  - Interest Rate: 1 percent per month
  - Loan Term: 10 months
  - Arrangement Fee: 2 percent of loan amount = 2 percent × £135,000 = £2,700

- ○ Exit Fee: 1 percent of loan amount = 1 percent × £135,000 = £1,350
- ○ Total Interest: 1 percent × £135,000 × 10 months = £13,500
- ○ Total Finance Costs: £2,700 (arrangement fee) + £1,350 (exit fee) + £13,500 (interest) = £17,550

Projected Rental Income

- Number of Rentable Rooms: Six
- Monthly Rent per Room: £400
- Total Monthly Rental Income: 6 × £400 = £2,400
- Total Yearly Rental Income Over 12 Months: £2,400 × 12 = £28,800 (this is net since housing authorities usually pay most of the running expenses)

Operating Expenses

Since the property is rented under a social housing scheme, most operational costs are covered by the housing provider. The investor's expenses are minimal.

- Council tax: £1,000
- Insurance: £500 pro-rated
- HMO compliance (visits, licence): £500
- Total Operating Expenses: £1,000 (council tax) + £500 (insurance) + £500 (compliance) = £2,000

Future Property Valuation Based on 10 Percent Net Yield
To determine the future sale price, the property is valued based on a 10 percent net yield of its annualized NOI (net operating income).

- Annualized NOI:
  - ○ £26,800 for a year (£28,800 − £2,000)
- Future Property Value:
  - ○ Property Value = Annual NOI ÷ Net Yield
  - ○ £26,800 ÷ 0.10 = £268,000

Total Costs and Profit Calculation

1. Total Costs Incurred by the Investor
   - Initial Cash Investment: £45,000
   - Closing costs: £10,000
   - Finance Costs: £17,550
   - Operating Expenses during holding period: £2,000
   - Total Costs Before Sale:
     - £45,000 + £17,550 + £2,000 + £10,000 = £74,550
2. Sale of the Property
   - Sale Price: £268,000
   - Selling Costs:
     - Estate Agent Fees: 2 percent × £268,000 = £5,360
     - Legal Fees: £1,500
     - Total Selling Costs: £5,360 + £1,500 = £6,860
3. Net Proceeds from Sale
   - Gross Sale Proceeds: £268,000
   - Less Selling Costs: £268,000 − £6,860 = £261,140
   - Less Loan Repayment: £261,140 − £135,000 = £126,140
4. Profit Before Taxes
   - Net Profit: Net Proceeds − Total Costs Before Sale
     - £126,140 − £74,550 = £51,590
5. Return on Investment (ROI)
   - ROI Calculation: £51,590 / 55,000 (initial capital + closing costs) = 93 percent (in 10 months)

Analysis

By initially investing £45,000 and using bridging finance, the investor achieves a net profit of £51,590 in just 10 months. The ROI (including holding costs and other closing costs) of approximately 93 percent highlights the effectiveness of leveraging financing in property investments, especially when associated with HMO developments.

Risk Assessment and Mitigation:

- Market Demand: Social housing schemes often have high demand, reducing the risk of vacancies.

- Fixed Rental Income: Long-term contracts with housing providers ensure stable income.
- Operational Efficiency: Minimal management required as the housing provider handles most responsibilities.
- Regulatory Compliance: Upfront investment in meeting HMO standards mitigates legal risks.
- Local housing authorities have social and political objectives, making them at risk of political volatility. Understanding their priorities is important to plan for potential political shifts.

Tax Considerations:

- Capital Gains Tax (CGT): Profit from the sale may be subject to CGT.
- Stamp Duty Land Tax (SDLT): Applicable on the purchase price.
- Professional Advice: Consulting with a tax adviser is recommended to optimize tax liabilities.

Conclusion

By strategically leveraging bridging finance and partnering with a social housing provider, the investor significantly enhances profitability while minimizing operational burdens. With a rental income of £400 per room, the property appreciates in value due to increased NOI, allowing for a lucrative exit strategy.

3.5 Bridging Finance for Owner-Occupiers

While bridging finance is primarily associated with investment projects, it can also benefit **owner-occupiers** seeking to purchase a new home before selling their existing property. In such scenarios, bridging loans offer a convenient stopgap for homeowners who need temporary funds to finalize the purchase of a new residence. By bridging the financial gap between two transactions, owner-occupiers avoid the logistical challenges—and potential disappointments—that can arise when attempting to coordinate simultaneous property sales and purchases.

1. **Securing the New Property Quickly**

   Owner-occupiers who discover an ideal home may hesitate if they have not yet sold their current residence. A bridging loan allows them to proceed with the new purchase immediately, rather than losing out on the property to another buyer. This immediate availability of capital is often worth the short-term higher interest, especially in competitive markets where desirable listings move quickly.

2. **Bridging the Gap Between Transactions**

   Because the owner-occupier's existing home typically has substantial equity, the sale proceeds can later be used to repay the bridging loan. Once the original residence is sold, any outstanding bridging debt is cleared, and the homeowner can decide whether to move to a long-term mortgage on the new property. This approach streamlines both sales and purchases, making it less likely that a potential buyer will withdraw due to prolonged waiting periods.

3. **Avoiding Double Moves**

   Without bridging finance, owner-occupiers who sell first may need temporary accommodation or risk missing the window on their dream home. By contrast, having a bridging loan in place allows them to move directly from one property to the other. The convenience of avoiding an interim rental property, combined with a reduced risk of broken chains, often outweighs the additional cost of short-term financing.

Key considerations for owner-occupiers are:

Regulated Bridging and Affordability Checks:

When bridging finance is secured against a main residence, the loan may fall under Financial Conduct Authority (FCA) regulations, meaning lenders typically conduct affordability and suitability assessments. Although these checks can make the process more rigorous than unregulated (investment) bridging, they also provide owner-occupiers with an extra layer of consumer protection and clarity regarding terms.

Timeline and Exit Strategy:

A prompt sale of the current home remains vital to control interest costs. While bridging can ease timing pressures, extended delays in selling the original property can lead to higher overall expenses. Consequently, owner-occupiers should carefully evaluate local market conditions, prepare their property for sale, and maintain realistic expectations about the time frame for repaying the bridging loan.

Overall, bridging finance serves as a strategic solution for owner-occupiers who have sufficient equity, a solid repayment plan, and a clear understanding of the short-term costs involved. By enabling them to secure a new home before their old one sells, bridging finance helps homeowners navigate a complex real estate market with greater speed and confidence.

3.6 Using Bridging Finance for Title Splitting

Title splitting is a property investment strategy where a single property (usually a building) is divided into multiple titles, allowing the investor to sell individual units separately. This approach can significantly enhance the overall value of the property, as individual units often command higher prices when sold separately compared to selling the property as a whole. Bridging finance can play a critical role in facilitating this process by providing the short-term funding required to acquire, subdivide, and prepare the property for resale.

Key Steps in Title Splitting with Bridging Finance:

1. **Acquisition of the Property**

   Bridging finance is commonly used to purchase properties suitable for title splitting, such as large houses, apartment buildings, or commercial spaces with the potential for conversion into multiple units. Since these properties may not qualify for traditional mortgages due to their size, condition, or existing use, bridging loans provide a quick and flexible funding solution. You can use property websites such as Zoopla or Rightmove and search the keyword "title split" (you need to use double quotation marks to search both words together).

2. **Legal and Survey Work**

   Once the property is acquired, legal and survey work is undertaken to divide the title into separate units. This involves working with solicitors and surveyors to prepare the necessary documentation, including new title deeds, floor plans, and legal boundaries for each unit. Bridging finance can cover the costs of these services, ensuring the process is completed efficiently.

3. **Renovation and Conversion**

   Investors often need to renovate or convert the property to make each unit suitable for sale. For example, a large house might be converted into self-contained flats, or a commercial building might be reconfigured into residential units. Bridging loans can finance these renovation costs, often through staged disbursements tied to project milestones.

4. **Sale of Individual Units**

   Once the units are legally divided and ready for sale, they can be marketed individually. Selling the units separately typically yields a higher combined sale price than selling the property as a single entity. The proceeds from the sales can then be used to repay the bridging loan and generate profit for the investor.

Victorian Townhouse Conversion

An investor purchased a large Victorian townhouse in Manchester for £600,000. The property had four floors and was in good structural condition but was outdated in terms of internal layout and amenities. The plan was to split it into four self-contained flats, which would increase its value significantly. This area of Manchester has high demand for flats due to its proximity to the city center and universities, making it an ideal investment for title splitting.

Experience with Bridging Finance

Given the competitive nature of the market, the investor needed to act quickly to secure the property. He opted for a bridging loan with a 12-month term, allowing flexibility while we handled the title-splitting process and renovations. The bridging loan provided 75 percent of the purchase price (£450,000) and covered a portion of the refurbishment costs, allowing the investor to start the project immediately.

The loan's flexibility allowed him to roll up interest payments, so he didn't have to worry about monthly payments while the project was underway. This was particularly useful, as the planning permission and title-splitting process took longer than expected—around 5 months in total. The flexibility of the bridging loan enabled him to manage this delay without financial strain.

Numbers Involved

- Purchase price: £600,000.
- Bridging loan: £450,000 (LTV 75 percent).
- Interest rate: 0.9 percent per month.
- Total loan fees: £9,000 (2 percent arrangement fee) and £3,000 in legal fees.
- Total refurbishment and splitting costs: £120,000 (including £45,000 for planning permission and legal title-splitting fees, £55,000 for internal layout changes, and £20,000 for new kitchens and bathrooms in each flat).
- Loan interests for 5 months: £20,250
- Sale price of each flat: £200,000 (total: £800,000).
- Total costs: £20,250 (interests) + £3,000 legal fees + £9,000 arrangement fees + £120,000 conversion costs + £600,000 purchase price = £752,250
- Total pre-tax profit: £47,750 (ROI on £302,250 capital employed, 16 percent, or 38 percent annualized excluding selling costs which might cost around £8,000).

Conclusion

The use of bridging finance allowed the investor to act quickly, secure the property, and fund the renovation and title-splitting process. Despite the delay in planning permission, the rolled-up interest structure ensured he could stay focused on the project without worrying about monthly payments. The project was a success, resulting in a significant profit after the sale of all four flats.

Benefits of Using Bridging Finance for Title Splitting

- **Quick Access to Funds**: Enables investors to secure properties that may otherwise be unavailable due to time constraints or condition.
- **Flexibility**: Funds can be used not only for acquisition but also for legal, survey, and renovation costs.
- **Enhanced Returns**: Selling units individually can significantly increase the total value of the property.

Risks and Considerations

- **Legal and Planning Challenges**: Title splitting requires compliance with local planning regulations, which can vary by area. Investors should work with experienced solicitors and surveyors to navigate these requirements.
- **Market Conditions**: The success of this strategy depends on strong demand for the subdivided units. Thorough market research is essential to ensure profitability.
- **Exit Strategy**: Delays in selling individual units can increase bridging loan costs, so investors must have a clear and realistic sales timeline.

Conclusion: Bridging Finance as a Strategic Tool

Bridging finance offers property investors—and occasionally owner-occupiers—the flexibility and speed needed to capitalize on a wide range of opportunities, from auction purchases to property flipping, conversions, and even the transitional purchase of a new home before selling an old one. Whether you're looking to buy, renovate, or refinance, bridging loans provide a fast, efficient way to secure the necessary funds.

The key to success with bridging finance is having a clear exit strategy—whether through refinancing with a traditional mortgage or selling the property after completion. At Integer Investments, we help investors structure their bridging loans in a way that maximizes returns while minimizing risks. In the next chapter, we'll explore the mechanics of bridging loans, including interest rates, fees, and how to structure an agreement that works for your investment goals.

CHAPTER 4

How Bridging Loans Work for Property Investors

Understanding how bridging loans are structured, including loan-to-value (LTV) ratios, interest rates, and the associated costs, is crucial for any property investor. A well-structured bridging loan allows investors to take advantage of short-term opportunities while managing risks effectively. In this chapter, we'll break down the key financial mechanics of bridging loans and how to optimize them for property investments.

4.1 Loan-to-Value Ratios and Interest Rates

The **LTV ratio** is a critical factor in bridging loans. It represents the amount of the loan as a percentage of the property's value, typically calculated based on either the purchase price or the current market value. For instance, if an investor is purchasing a property worth £100,000 with an LTV of 75 percent, they can borrow up to £75,000. Lenders assess the LTV ratio to determine the level of risk involved in issuing the loan, with lower LTV ratios indicating less risk for the lender (and usually demanding lower interest rates).

In the UK, most lenders cap their LTV ratios between **60 and 75 percent**. However, some lenders, such as Integer Investments, offer LTV ratios of **up to 85 percent** for experienced investors with a strong track record. This allows investors to leverage more capital, enabling them to complete projects with minimal upfront costs. Higher LTVs can be beneficial for investors, but they often come with higher interest rates as they represent a higher risk to the lender.

Interest rates for bridging loans are another key component, typically ranging from **0.75 to 1.5 percent per month**, depending on the lender and the borrower's financial standing. These rates are significantly higher than traditional mortgages due to the short-term nature and associated risks of bridging loans. For example, an investor taking out a loan at 1 percent per month would pay 12 percent interest annually.

In some scenarios, a second-charge bridging finance can actually be more cost-effective than refinancing a conventional mortgage—despite its higher monthly interest rate. For instance, imagine an investor owns a buy-to-let (BTL) property worth £1 million, with a £500,000 mortgage at 2.5 percent annually. The investor wants to release £100,000 of equity for a new acquisition, but refinancing the entire loan would increase the interest rate to 5.5 percent. Consequently, the annual interest bill would jump from £12,500 to £33,000, meaning the extra £100,000 effectively carries an interest cost exceeding 20 percent per year.

By contrast, if the investor keeps the existing mortgage at 2.5 percent and raises £100,000 through a bridge loan charging 1 percent per month plus a 2 percent fee, the total additional cost would be £12,000 in yearly interest plus £2,000 in fees. In this scenario, the investor saves around £6,500 over a 12-month period compared to the cost of fully refinancing at 5.5 percent (assuming legal costs are equivalent between the two scenarios).

Interest can be structured in various ways:

1. Monthly Interest Payments

With **monthly interest** payments, the borrower makes regular interest payments over the life of the loan, while the principal is typically repaid at the end of the term.

- **How It Works**
  Suppose an investor borrows **£200,000** at **1 percent** monthly interest for **6 months**.
  - Monthly interest due: 1 percent of £200,000 = **£2,000**.
  - These £2,000 payments are made each month for 6 months, totaling **£12,000** in interest.
  - At the end of 6 months, the borrower repays the original £200,000 principal.
- **Pros**
  - The loan balance remains stable because interest isn't added on top of the principal.
  - Avoids a large lump-sum interest payment at the end of the term.

- **Cons**
  - Requires consistent cash flow to meet monthly interest obligations.
  - If the project is delayed or revenue is lower than expected, covering monthly payments can be challenging.

2. Rolled-Up Interest

With **rolled-up interest**, no interest payments are made during the term. Instead, the interest accrues ("rolls up") and is repaid along with the principal at redemption.

- **How It Works**

  Consider a **£200,000** loan at **1 percent** monthly interest over **6 months**, with the interest rolled up.
  - Total interest for 6 months: 1 percent $\times$ £200,000 $\times$ 6 = **£12,000**.
  - At redemption (end of 6 months), the borrower repays **£212,000** (the original £200,000 plus £12,000 in accrued interest).
- **Pros**
  - No monthly payments, which can be helpful if the property is undergoing renovation and not yet generating income.
  - Simplified accounting, as interest is settled in one lump sum.
- **Cons**
  - The loan balance grows each month as interest accrues, so the final repayment can be large.
  - Some lenders reduce the maximum LTV to account for the higher payoff amount at maturity.

3. Retained Interest

Retained interest is deducted in advance from the total loan. You receive less cash on day 1, but no ongoing payments are required, and you only owe the principal at the end.

- **How It Works**

  Assume an investor borrows **£200,000** for **6 months** at **1 percent** monthly interest, plus a **2 percent arrangement fee**. The lender

calculates total interest for 6 months (1 percent × £200,000 ×
6 = £12,000) and retains it upfront.

- The borrower effectively receives **£188,000** at closing
  (£200,000 − £12,000 interest).
- If there's also a 2 percent arrangement fee (£4,000), the net
  amount disbursed could drop to **£184,000**.
- At redemption, the borrower pays back **£200,000** in principal
  (the interest was already "retained"), assuming no extension or
  late fees.

- **Pros**
  - No monthly interest payments; the borrower can focus on
    renovation or other project costs.
  - Certainty about interest costs: They are fixed and accounted
    for from the start.
- **Cons**
  - Reduced day 1 funding because the interest is withheld
    initially.
  - If the project finishes early, the borrower may have effec-
    tively prepaid interest for unused months, depending on the
    lender's terms. In some cases, lenders reimburse "unused"
    interest.
  - The retained nature of interest effectively increases the costs
    of capital.

Choosing the Right Structure

Selecting a payment structure depends on the borrower's **cash-flow
requirements**, the **project timeline**, and the **lender's criteria**. Investors
with strong monthly revenue might opt for monthly payments to keep
the final repayment smaller, while those who need maximum capital for
renovations may prefer rolled-up or retained interest, despite the higher
final payoff or reduced initial loan proceeds.

4.2 Fees and Costs Associated with Bridging Loans

In addition to interest rates, bridging loans come with several fees and
costs that investors must account for. These can significantly impact the

total cost of borrowing and should be factored into the investment's profitability calculations.

- **Arrangement Fee**: This is typically charged by the lender for setting up the loan and usually ranges from **1 to 2 percent** of the loan amount. For example, on a £200,000 loan, an arrangement fee of 1.5 percent would amount to £3,000.
- **Valuation Fee**: A property valuation is required to determine the loan amount and assess the property's market value. The valuation fee varies depending on the property's size and value but typically ranges from **£300 to £1,500**. Some lenders prefer in-person surveyors while others accept virtual or desktop valuations, with the latter being cheaper and faster to conduct.
- **Legal Fees**: Both the borrower and the lender need legal representation to complete the loan agreement. The borrower is usually responsible for covering both sets of legal fees, which can range from **£1,000 to £2,000**, depending on the complexity of the transaction. For larger transactions, costs can go up significantly.
- **Exit Fee**: Some lenders charge an exit fee when the loan is repaid. This is typically a percentage of the loan amount, often **around 1 percent**.
- **Extension Fees**: If the borrower is unable to repay the loan within the agreed term, an extension fee may be applied. This can range from **3 to 5 percent of the loan amount**, which can significantly increase the cost of the project.

Investors need to budget for these fees upfront to ensure their project remains profitable. In general, these fees can comprise half of the total costs for a bridge loan. Therefore, if an investor underestimates these costs, they may find their returns diminished, especially if the project timeline extends beyond the original term.

4.3 Structuring a Bridging Loan Agreement

The structure of a bridging loan agreement can vary significantly depending on the lender, the borrower's financial situation, and the property in question. A well-structured agreement allows the investor to maximize the loan's benefits while minimizing costs and risks.

Key considerations include:

- **Loan Term**: Most bridging loans have a term between 6 and 12 months. For example, Integer Investments typically offers loans with terms ranging from **4 to 18 months**, depending on the project type. It's essential for investors to have a clear exit strategy to avoid extension fees.
- **Repayment Options**: As mentioned earlier, investors can choose between monthly interest payments, rolled-up interest, or retained interest. The choice depends on the investor's cash flow and how quickly they expect to complete the project or secure refinancing.
- **Exit Strategy**: The exit strategy is a critical part of the loan agreement. Whether through selling the property or refinancing with a mortgage, the exit strategy must be clear to both the borrower and lender. Failing to adhere to the exit plan can result in additional costs or, in extreme cases, foreclosure.

For example, an investor planning to flip a property within six months might opt for a rolled-up interest structure, as they won't need to worry about monthly payments during the renovation phase. Once the property is sold, they can use the proceeds to repay the loan and the accrued interest.

4.4 Cross-Collateralization in Bridging Loans

Cross-collateralization refers to the practice of using multiple properties (or other valuable assets) as security for a single bridging facility. Rather than pledging just one property, the borrower grants the lender legal charges over two or more properties, thereby increasing the combined pool of collateral. This approach can be beneficial in situations where:

- A single property's value isn't sufficient to support the desired loan amount.

- The borrower aims to raise more capital at a higher effective loan-to-value (LTV) across multiple properties.
- The borrower owns several properties, each with equity, but none individually meet the lender's underwriting criteria for the total sum required.

Following are the key points to consider when employing cross-collateralization within a bridging finance arrangement.

4.4.1 Why Cross-Collateralize?

1. **Higher Aggregate LTV**
   By combining multiple properties as collateral, an investor can boost the overall security value and qualify for a larger bridging loan. For example, suppose the investor wants to buy a £200,000 property but has no available capital. A bridging lender agrees to finance 70 percent of the purchase price, leaving a £60,000 short-fall. Fortunately, the investor also owns a second property valued at £300,000 with an outstanding mortgage of £150,000. By borrowing up to 70 percent of that property's £300,000 value (£210,000), then subtracting the existing £150,000 mortgage, the investor can free up the extra £60,000 needed for the new acquisition. Adding a second property can raise the total accessible capital without exceeding the lender's maximum overall LTV.

2. **Unlocking Additional Equity**
   Investors with partial equity spread across several assets can consolidate this equity under one bridging facility, potentially speeding up the transaction. Instead of arranging separate loans for each property, cross-collateralization simplifies the financing structure into a single facility.

3. **Rapid Portfolio Transactions**
   In some scenarios—such as the rapid purchase of multiple buy-to-let properties at auction—cross-collateralization can provide the liquidity needed to seize deals quickly. Borrowers leverage the entire portfolio's equity rather than piecemeal with each property, streamlining the process.

4.4.2 How It Works in Practice

1. **Valuations on Each Property**
   The lender orders separate valuations to determine each property's individual market worth. Based on these valuations, the lender calculates the maximum aggregated lending limit. Typically, they still impose a maximum LTV (e.g., 65 to 75 percent) on the combined portfolio's value.

2. **Legal Charges over Multiple Assets**
   The lender registers first- or second-charge mortgages against each property, depending on whether an existing mortgage or charge is already in place. If any property is unencumbered (no existing mortgage), a first charge can be obtained easily. If not, a second-charge bridging arrangement might be used, subject to the first lender's consent.

3. **Single Loan Agreement**
   Although several properties are pledged, the borrower often signs a single bridging facility agreement. The "security schedule" lists all assets included as collateral. The total loan amount, interest rate, fees, and exit strategy are addressed in one overarching contract.

4. **Exit Strategy Across Multiple Properties**
   Borrowers need to outline a clear plan to repay the bridging loan. This may involve selling one of the pledged properties, refinancing the entire portfolio, or a combination (e.g., selling two properties and refinancing the remainder). If the intention is to sell, the lender usually requires partial repayment each time a property is disposed of, reducing the outstanding loan balance proportionally.

4.4.3 Benefits and Drawbacks

Benefits:

1. **Increased Borrowing Power**
   Borrowers can unlock additional funds by aggregating property values—useful for major renovations or multiple acquisitions needing substantial capital.

2. **Potentially Lower Overall Cost**
   In some cases, a single bridging facility (cross-collateralized) might cost less in total arrangement fees than multiple stand-alone loans, each with separate fees and legal costs.
3. **Portfolio-Level Flexibility**
   Borrowers can manage refurbishment or development projects across various properties, drawing on the combined equity rather than juggling separate loan accounts.

Drawbacks:

1. **Higher Risk to the Borrower**
   If the borrower defaults, the lender can enforce security on any or all pledged properties. Even if only one property underperforms or fails to sell, the entire portfolio is at stake.
2. **Complex Legal Process**
   Multiple valuations, legal checks, and charges over several assets can lengthen the due diligence phase. Borrowers should factor in extra conveyancing time and costs.
3. **Restricted Future Borrowing**
   Cross-collateralizing can tie up equity in multiple properties. If the borrower wants to refinance or sell a single property in the group midterm, they may need the lender's permission, leading to partial releases of security and potential extension fees.

4.4.4 Practical Considerations:

1. **Transparency on Each Property**
   The lender typically requires full disclosure of any existing mortgages, leases, or known legal issues on each asset. The presence of tenants, sub-leases, or commercial elements can affect the aggregated LTV or interest rate offered.
2. **Partial Repayments and Security Releases**
   Borrowers who plan to sell one of the cross-collateralized properties during the bridging term should negotiate release terms at the outset. Typically, a lump-sum payment proportionate to that property's share of the loan is required before the lender removes its legal charge.

3. **Detailed Exit Strategy**

Lenders scrutinize the borrower's plan for each property, especially if each might have a distinct exit (e.g., flipping one, refinancing another, selling a third). The more intricate the plan, the more carefully the lender reviews the borrower's track record and timelines.

4. **Professional Advice**

The legal complexities of cross-collateralization warrant engaging experienced solicitors who are familiar with bridging transactions over multiple properties. This ensures a smoother process and helps avoid disputes over partial redemptions or title issues later.

4.4.5 Implications for Cross-Collateralizing an Owner-Occupier Property

Transforming into a Regulated Loan:
If an investor attempts to use both:

- **Property A**: An investment buy-to-let, and
- **Property B**: Their owner-occupied main home
  as security for a single bridging loan, the presence of the main residence typically **triggers regulated bridging**. In other words:
  - The lender either must be Financial Conduct Authority (FCA) authorized for regulated lending
  - Or must treat this as a regulated mortgage contract and comply with all associated consumer-protection rules.

Unregulated lenders—those specializing in purely commercial or business-purpose bridging—usually **cannot** or **will not** proceed if the loan is (even partly) secured against an owner-occupied home, as that brings them under an FCA scope for which they are not authorized.

Common Lender Policies:
Most bridging lenders have explicit policies:

1. **Regulated Lenders**: Will handle cross-collateralization even if it includes a main home, but with a regulated bridging contract.

2. **Unregulated Lenders**: Decline any arrangement securing a property used as the borrower's main residence.

Because cross-collateralization by definition merges the security pool into one loan, you cannot simply "carve out" the owner-occupier portion to keep the entire loan unregulated. The moment a main home is part of the collateral, the loan is effectively regulated.

4.4.6 Conclusion: Cross-Collateralization as a Strategic Tool

Cross-collateralization can significantly enhance an investor's borrowing power by pooling the equity from multiple properties under a single bridging loan. By allowing the lender to spread its security risk across a broader asset base, the borrower often secures a larger loan amount and greater flexibility than if they financed each property separately. However, this approach introduces higher stakes—defaulting on one property jeopardizes all pledged assets. Proper legal structuring, clear exit plans, and transparent communication with the lender are essential to ensure the benefits of cross-collateralization outweigh the potential risks.

4.5 Exit Strategies for Property Investors

Having a clear and viable **exit strategy** is essential when taking out a bridging loan. Without one, investors risk running into cash-flow problems or being forced to sell the property under unfavorable conditions.

Exit Strategy Optimization: The most common exit strategies for bridging loans involve either selling the property after renovation or refinancing it with a long-term mortgage and renting out the property. However, some investors adopt a more sophisticated approach, such as refinancing with a higher LTV mortgage after improvements have been made to the property, thus freeing up additional capital to invest elsewhere. This strategy, known as **re-leveraging**, allows investors to keep borrowing against the equity they create with each successful project, accelerating portfolio growth.

1. **Sale of the Property**: This is often the case in property flipping or development projects. The investor sells the property, repays the loan, and retains the profit.

2. **Refinancing with a Long-Term Mortgage**: Investors may refinance the property with a traditional buy-to-let or commercial mortgage after completing renovations or increasing the property's value. Refinancing is ideal for investors who want to retain the property and benefit from rental income or long-term capital appreciation. This **"buy, refurbish, rent, refinance"** (or BRRR) strategy allows investors to recycle their capital, using the equity gained from the improved property to fund subsequent investments. Investors who master this strategy can quickly expand their portfolios without needing substantial cash reserves for each project.

At **Integer Investments**, we emphasize the importance of a well-thought-out exit strategy when structuring our loans. For instance, we worked with an investor in London who used a bridging loan to purchase a property, renovate it, and then refinance with a buy-to-let mortgage within four months. The investor's clear exit strategy allowed them to minimize interest costs and maximize returns.

Conclusion: Mastering the Financial Mechanics of Bridging Loans

Bridging loans can be a powerful tool for property investors, but they require careful planning and a deep understanding of the associated costs, structures, and exit strategies. By considering key factors such as LTV ratios, interest rates, and fees, investors can structure loans in a way that maximizes profitability while minimizing risks.

It is important for bridge lenders to work closely with their clients to tailor bridging loans that suit their specific project needs. Whether it's flipping properties, developing new builds, or refinancing, having a solid understanding of how bridging loans work is essential to success in the UK property market.

In the next chapter, we'll explore the risks and challenges associated with bridging finance and how to navigate them effectively to ensure successful outcomes in property investments.

Case Study: HMO Conversion (By Derek Walczak)

My First Experience with a Bridging Loan: A Game-Changer for My Property Investment Journey

I did use a bridging loan for the first time to purchase a three-bedroom terraced property in St Helens, Northwest UK. The property was in such poor condition that it wasn't even habitable—no heating, no hot water, and no functional kitchen or bathroom. This is where the bridging loan became crucial. Properties in this state usually can't be financed through traditional buy-to-let mortgages, as lenders require basic amenities like heating, hot water, and functional bathrooms and kitchens. Often, different lenders have varying definitions of what "habitable" means, which can waste valuable time before discovering they won't lend on the property.

I purchased this property with confidence, knowing it met my size requirements for conversion into a house in multiple occupation (HMO). As with any HMO project, room sizes must adhere to strict guidelines, with most local authorities requiring a minimum of 6.51 m² for single occupancy bedrooms, although requirements can vary. My strategy was to buy a property needing significant refurbishment, as these offer great potential for adding value. I aimed to convert it into an HMO and secure a social housing lease.

The UK's housing crisis means that there's a growing demand in the social housing sector. I chose social housing because the lease structure is government backed. Landlords receive monthly rent for the lease's duration (which can range from 3 to 25 years), with the provider covering all bills and maintenance, except for structural repairs like roof damage. This model not only supports local housing needs but is also appealing to overseas investors looking for hands-off investments, especially since many are cash buyers.

The Bridging Loan Experience

From day 1, my bridging loan experience was positive. Many people don't realize the flexibility that bridging finance offers, especially in deals like mine. With quick access to funds and favorable interest rates, I could leverage my cash more effectively. For example, bridging loans can often cover up to 80 percent of a property's loan-to-value (LTV), allowing you to spread your funds across multiple projects, accelerating your growth.

However, I've also witnessed firsthand the challenges of selecting the wrong lender. A close friend of mine faced significant delays, shifting terms, and business losses due to poor service from his lender. Long story short, the lender required all fees to be paid upfront, which my friend did without hesitation. Despite this, it took the lender an additional 4 to 5 weeks to provide a decision in principle (DIP). Once we entered the conveyancing process, things only worsened—his solicitors would take an average of 7 to 10 days to respond to emails, leaving him feeling frustrated and neglected, as if no one cared about the outcome.

This experience taught me a valuable lesson: Choosing the right lender is critical. Thorough research and partnering with trusted professionals can make all the difference between a smooth transaction and one plagued by delays and unnecessary costs. Never underestimate the importance of working with a reliable, efficient team when financing property investments.

Overcoming the Challenge of a Corporate Sale

One of the biggest challenges I faced was completing a corporate sale, where speed is often essential. The property wasn't habitable, and the estate agents required a 14-day completion. Thanks to bridging finance, I secured the funds in days and completed the purchase swiftly. This experience underscored the value of bridging loans in fast-turnaround deals.

Financial Breakdown

Here's a snapshot of the financials for this investment:

- **Purchase Price**: £80,000 (80 percent LTV loan of £64,000 + £16,000 equity)
- **Refurbishment Costs**: £40,000 (100 percent financed)
  - Rewiring: £4,000
  - Kitchen: £3,000
  - Plastering/New Layout: £8,000
  - Fire Doors: £4,000
  - Bathrooms: £8,000
  - Decorating: £2,500
  - Flooring: £2,000
  - Furniture: £2,000
  - Waste Disposal: £1,500
  - Garden: £1,000
  - Heating System: £3,000
  - Inspections: £1,000
- **Other Costs (£5,700)**:
  - Stamp Duty: £2,400
  - Solicitors: £2,500
  - Survey/Valuation: £500
  - Insurance: £300

Total Investment including interests and fees: £131,940
Rental Income: £18,500 per annum (net)
Sale Price: £182,000
Profit: £50,060

The Exit Strategy

My exit strategy was to sell the property to an overseas investor with a secured social housing lease. This hands-off, income-generating model is particularly attractive to foreign buyers who are happy with the 10 percent net yield. At the same time, selling the property for a £50,000 profit was a significant achievement for myself.

Lessons Learned

This project taught me invaluable lessons about property financing. Years ago, a friend advised me to rely solely on savings for property purchases, but I've since learned that bridging finance is a more efficient way to scale. Working with lenders like Integer Investments enabled me to complete this project successfully and profitably.

CHAPTER 5

Risks and Challenges in Property Bridging Finance

Bridging finance offers many advantages for property investors, but it also comes with inherent risks. Navigating these challenges effectively requires a clear understanding of the potential pitfalls and how to mitigate them. In this chapter, we'll explore the common risks associated with bridging loans and provide practical strategies to minimize them.

5.1 Common Risks for Property Investors

While bridging finance can be a powerful tool for property investors, the short-term nature of these loans, coupled with high interest rates, means there are several risks that borrowers must be aware of:

- **Interest Rate Risk:** Bridging loans typically carry higher interest rates than traditional mortgages. Rates range from **0.75 to 1.5 percent per month**, which can add up quickly if the loan is extended beyond the initial term. If the project or exit strategy is delayed, this can significantly erode profits due to extension fees and longer time horizons.
- **Exit Strategy Failure:** The success of any bridging loan depends on a clear and viable exit strategy. If an investor's plan to refinance or sell the property falls through, they may face difficulties repaying the loan. This could lead to extension fees or, in worst cases, foreclosure on the property.
- **Market Volatility:** Property values can fluctuate, particularly in uncertain economic conditions. Investors relying on property appreciation for their exit strategy may find that market downturns erode the value of their investment, making it difficult to sell or

refinance at the expected price. In some cases (for example for HMO [house in multiple occupation] developers, nonresidents, or investors with large projects), banks change their lending criteria, making it harder to refinance. It is important to start discussions with banks or real estate agents well in advance to avoid surprises toward the end of the project.

- **Project Delays**: Renovation and development projects often encounter delays due to planning approvals, contractor availability, or unforeseen structural issues. In some cases, the presence of asbestos or other hazards can add substantial costs and delays. These delays can extend the loan term, leading to higher interest payments or extension fees.
- **Legal and Regulatory Risks**: Bridging loans often come with complex legal agreements. Investors must ensure that they fully understand the terms of the loan, including any hidden fees or penalties, to avoid costly surprises.

It is important for bridge lenders to help mitigate these risks by working closely with borrowers to ensure their projects have robust exit strategies and clear timelines.

Let me provide an example that brings together all these risks. It is unlikely to happen, but it is important to keep in mind that this is a real possibility.

Risk Example: Andrew's Flipping Project Gone Wrong

Andrew identifies what appears to be a lucrative flip—a property he can purchase for **£100,000**, renovate for **£25,000**, and then resell for **£160,000 to £170,000**. Confident in his estimates, he obtains a bridging loan at **75 percent loan to value (LTV)**, with **1 percent monthly interest**, a **2 percent arrangement fee**, and a **5 percent extension fee**. The lender advances **£93,750**, and Andrew plans to hold the property for **6 months**.

Initial Financial Breakdown

- **Purchase Price**: £100,000
- **Renovation Budget**: £25,000

- **Stamp Duty**: £5,000
- **Legal Fees (Purchase)**: £2,500
- **Bridging Finance Costs**: £7,500 (£5,625 interest over 6 months + £1,875 arrangement fee)

Adding everything, Andrew anticipates spending **£140,000** total, including his equity contribution of **£46,250** to cover the shortfall and associated fees. He aims to sell the property for **£170,000**, with estimated selling costs of **£3,500** (agent + legals), leaving him **£166,500** net. That sets his projected profit at **£26,500**—an impressive **57 percent return** on his 6-month investment, which annualizes to over 100 percent.

Unexpected Renovation Costs

Shortly after starting work, Andrew discovers:

- **Leaking Roof**: Repair cost of **£8,000**
- **Asbestos Removal**: Remediation costs of **£5,000**

These unforeseen expenses raise his renovation budget from £25,000 to **£38,000**. Fortunately, Andrew's parents can lend him the extra funds, and he still expects to see roughly **£13,000** in profit. However, fixing these problems extends the project timeline by **3 months**, pushing it to **9 months**. Consequently, Andrew must also pay 3 additional months of bridging interest.

Market Downturn and Rising Interest Rates

Mid-renovation, the UK government faces economic headwinds, driving government bond yields higher. Mortgage rates climb from **4 to 6 percent**, causing a **5 percent drop** in local property values. Andrew revises his selling price down to **£160,000**, leaving him less room for profit—but he still hopes to break even.

Delays and Extension Fees

After listing the property, Andrew struggles to find a buyer. There is political uncertainty, talk of higher stamp duty levies, and many buyers become cautious. As he approaches **12 months**, the bridging lender demands repayment. With no sale in sight, Andrew faces a **5 percent extension fee**—paid upfront—if he wants more time. He cannot raise additional capital for this fee, leaving him in a tight spot.

Fire Sale and Final Outcome

Lacking better options, Andrew resorts to a **fire sale** at **£140,000**—two months past his original loan deadline. This means he has held the property for **14 months** and ultimately suffers a significant loss of capital. The final numbers are:

- **Selling Price**: £140,000
- **Purchase Price**: £100,000
- **Renovation**: £38,000
- **Bridging Interest**: £13,125
- **Arrangement Fee**: £1,875
- **Extension Fee**: £4,688
- **Purchase Legals**: £2,500
- **Stamp Duty**: £5,000
- **Selling Agent Fees**: £2,500
- **Selling Legals**: £1,000

Total Costs: £168,688
Resulting "Profit": −£28,688

Conclusion

Andrew's experience illustrates how unforeseen construction expenses, market volatility, rising interest rates, and extended hold times can combine to derail even the most promising flip. His reliance on tight forecasts—and lack of contingency funds—magnified the impact of each setback. This cautionary tale underscores the importance of **realistic budgets, robust exit strategies,** and **thorough contingency planning** in bridging-financed property deals.

Some investors may believe that the convergence of so many unfavorable factors is improbable. However, each event—unexpected renovations, a cooling market, spiking interest rates, and difficulty selling—has indeed occurred in recent years. Andrew's outcome demonstrates that, while profitable flips are possible, borrowers must be prepared for multiple worst-case scenarios to protect their investment and avoid catastrophic losses.

5.2 Maximizing Leverage

Bridging finance can also be used strategically to maximize leverage—borrowing more to increase potential returns. For experienced investors with a solid track record, lenders like Integer Investments may offer higher LTV ratios (up to 85 percent), allowing them to take on more ambitious projects. While higher leverage can lead to greater profits, it also increases risk, so investors need to carefully assess market conditions and have a clear exit strategy to avoid financial strain. For instance, an investor with £60,000 could purchase a property worth £200,000 using a bridge lender offering 70 percent LTV, covering £140,000. The investor would need to provide £60,000 for the deposit (in addition to closing costs), and thus could only purchase one property. Alternatively, with a lender offering 85 percent LTV, the investor would need just £30,000 per property, enabling them to buy two houses with the same capital. Increased leverage has the potential to boost returns (see scenario 1) but also increases risks in a downturn situation (see scenario 2).

Scenario 1: Property Prices Increase by 10 Percent:

- **Seventy Percent LTV (One Property)**: If property values rise by 10 percent, the single house's value increases to £220,000, giving the investor a profit of £20,000 on their investment, equal to 33 percent ROE.
- **Eighty-Five Percent LTV (Two Properties)**: With two properties worth £200,000 each, both now rise to £220,000, meaning the investor gains £40,000 in total—doubling their profit from leveraging higher LTV and purchasing two homes, equal to 66 percent

ROE. This illustrates how using higher leverage can significantly enhance returns during a property price appreciation phase.

Scenario 2: Property Prices Decrease by 10 Percent:

- **Seventy Percent LTV (One Property)**: A 10 percent price drop would reduce the house value to £180,000. The investor's equity shrinks, with a paper loss of £20,000, though the property's long-term potential could still be intact. The potential loss of capital equals 33 percent.

- **Eighty-Five Percent LTV (Two Properties)**: With two properties, both worth £200,000 originally, their value drops to £180,000 each. The total loss across both properties would be £40,000, or 66 percent of initial capital. In this case, higher leverage increases risk exposure, as the larger loan and lower equity cushion make the investor more vulnerable to market downturns. With declining prices, they could face difficulty refinancing or selling without incurring a loss.

5.3 Pitfalls to Avoid in the UK Property Market

There are several common pitfalls that investors should avoid when using bridging finance in the UK property market. Recognizing these early can help investors make more informed decisions and avoid costly mistakes:

- **Underestimating Costs**: Many investors make the mistake of underestimating the total costs involved in their project. In addition to the property purchase and renovation costs, there are fees associated with the loan itself, including arrangement, legal, valuation, and exit fees. Failing to budget for these costs can lead to financial strain.

- **Overleveraging**: Investors who take on too much debt relative to the property's value or their overall financial situation may find themselves overleveraged. If property values fall or the project encounters delays, the investor could struggle to repay the loan. Keeping LTV ratios conservative can help mitigate this risk.

- **Choosing the Wrong Lender:** Not all lenders are created equal. Investors should carefully evaluate lenders based on their interest rates, fees, and overall reputation. A lender with hidden fees or unfavorable terms could turn a profitable project into a financial burden.
- **Lack of a Contingency Plan:** Every project should have a contingency plan in place. This could include having additional funds available to cover unforeseen costs or having a secondary exit strategy in case the initial plan to refinance or sell the property falls through.

Conclusion: Managing Risks in Bridging Finance

While bridging finance offers considerable benefits for property investors, it also carries risks that must be carefully managed. By fully understanding the costs involved, maintaining conservative LTV ratios, and having a clear exit strategy, investors can minimize their exposure to potential pitfalls. Additionally, working with reputable lenders ensures that the terms of the loan are transparent and aligned with the borrower's goals.

In the next chapter, we'll delve into the legal and regulatory aspects of bridging finance in the UK, providing insights into how to navigate the complex legal landscape surrounding these loans.

CHAPTER 6

Choosing the Right Bridging Finance Lender

The choice of lender is critical in bridging finance, as the terms, conditions, and overall experience can vary significantly across providers. A good lender can help ensure a smooth, profitable investment, while the wrong choice can result in delays, unexpected fees, and financial strain. In this chapter, we'll explore the key factors to consider when selecting a bridging finance lender and how to evaluate their terms to secure the best deal for your project.

6.1 Evaluating Lenders in the UK Market

The UK bridging finance market is highly competitive, with numerous lenders offering a variety of loan products. Some lenders specialize in small projects, while others focus on larger developments. It's important to identify the lender whose product offerings align with your specific needs.

Here are some key types of lenders you'll encounter:

- **Specialist Bridging Lenders**: These lenders focus exclusively on bridging finance and are usually more flexible and experienced in handling complex property transactions. They often offer a wider range of products and can tailor loans to fit individual investor needs. Integer Investments, for example, specializes in bridging loans for property investors, offering flexible terms and fast approvals to meet market demands.
- **High-Street Banks**: Traditional banks also offer bridging loans, but their approval processes can be slower, and their terms may be more rigid. High-street banks often require a higher level of

security and tend to cater to more conservative lending profiles, which may not suit investors needing fast, flexible financing.

- **Private Lenders**: Private lenders provide a personalized lending approach. These lenders may be willing to take on higher-risk projects in exchange for higher interest rates. Investors should proceed with caution, as terms can be less regulated, and fees may be less transparent. Different lenders will also have various levels of professionalism and might not be borrower-friendly if problems arise.
- **Peer-to-peer (P2P) lending platforms:** Online entities connect individual investors with borrowers, bypassing traditional financial institutions. In the bridging finance space, these platforms offer quick access to funds and often provide flexible terms, but they can carry higher interest rates due to the risk profile. P2P platforms may also have less stringent credit requirements, making them an attractive option for investors who may not qualify for traditional loans. However, as with private lending, transparency can vary, and borrowers should review all terms carefully. As an example, CrowdProperty (www.crowdproperty.com) is a UK-based platform specializing in property-backed loans, including bridging finance. It connects borrowers, such as property developers and investors, with individual lenders who fund the loans.

When evaluating lenders, consider the following:

- **Speed of Approval**: How quickly can the lender approve your loan? For auction purchases, you may need a lender that can approve and disburse funds within days.
- **Flexibility**: Does the lender offer flexible repayment terms, such as rolled-up or retained interest? Can they accommodate extension requests if the project is delayed?
- **Reputation**: Research the lender's reputation by reading reviews and case studies. A reputable lender will have a history of transparent practices and a track record of successfully funding similar projects.
- When evaluating bridging loan options, investors should consider not only the interest rates but also the **total cost of the**

loan, which includes additional fees. While bridging loan interest rates typically range from **0.75 to 1.5 percent per month**, other costs—such as **arrangement fees** (usually 1 to 2 percent), valuation fees, and legal fees—can significantly increase the overall expense. To gain a clear picture of affordability, it's essential to account for all associated charges, including **exit fees** and **extension fees**, which can arise if the loan period needs to be prolonged.

Understanding the real cost difference can make a substantial impact. For instance, on a **£100,000 loan over six months**, the difference between an interest rate of **0.85 percent** and **1.0 percent** per month equates to an additional **£150 per month**, or **£900** over the loan's term. This increase is roughly equivalent to a **1 percent higher arrangement fee**. Some lenders also charge fees for disbursing funds, issuing documents and other tasks. Although these fees are generally small, they can add up quickly.

However, while cost is an important factor, it's not the only consideration. **Speed and reliability** can often outweigh minor differences in costs, especially in time-sensitive scenarios such as property acquisitions or auction purchases. Investors should balance affordability with the assurance that the lender can deliver funds quickly and reliably when needed.

By carefully evaluating both the financial and practical aspects of a bridging loan, investors can make informed decisions that align with their specific objectives.

6.2 Understanding Terms and Conditions

The terms and conditions of a bridging loan can make or break an investment. It's essential to fully understand every aspect of the loan agreement before proceeding. The following are key terms you should carefully review:

- **Interest Rates**: Bridging loan interest rates are typically higher than those of traditional mortgages. Rates can range from **0.75 to 1.5 percent per month**, depending on the lender and the borrower's profile. Compare rates across lenders to ensure you're getting a competitive deal. Online, various tools are available to compare loans of different kinds. Integer Investments provides one for free on its website.

- **Fees**: Lenders often charge a range of fees in addition to the interest rate. Common fees include arrangement fees, valuation fees, legal fees, and exit fees. Most lenders charge around **2 percent as an arrangement fee**, with about 1 percent in exit fees. Other lenders may have more complex fee structures, so ensure you understand the total cost of the loan.

- **Loan-to-Value (LTV) Ratio**: The LTV ratio represents the amount you can borrow against the value of the property. Lenders typically offer LTV ratios between **60 percent and 75 percent**, but for experienced investors with good credit, some lenders may offer LTVs up to **85 percent**. Higher LTVs allow you to borrow more but may come with higher interest rates or stricter conditions. However, make sure you understand the net loan. Some lenders deduct all fees and costs in advance. So a 70 percent LTV might actually disburse only 65 percent after all deductions, so an investor needs a larger deposit.

- **Loan Term**: Bridging loans are short term, typically lasting **4 to 18 months**. It's important to select a term that aligns with your project timeline. Consider whether the lender allows for extensions and what fees may apply if the project is delayed. And, most importantly, the extension is in the hands of the lender and, in some cases, they might refuse an extension, creating significant problems for the borrower.

- **Other Conditions**: Some lenders impose additional conditions beyond standard terms. These can include:
  - **Repaying an Existing Loan**: Some bridging lenders may require borrowers to clear any existing debts on the property before disbursing the loan.
  - **Conducting Additional Searches**: Depending on the property type, lenders may request additional due diligence, such as conducting asbestos surveys, structural assessments, or environmental checks.
  - **Additional documents**: Lenders might ask you to prove your income, or proof of ownership of other properties, or sign a renovation contract with a builder with a precise quote and estimate.

- ○ **Cash Reserves:** Lenders may require the borrower to have a certain amount of cash reserves as a buffer for unforeseen expenses, ensuring the project doesn't run into financial difficulties midway.
- ○ **Development Progress Milestones:** In development projects, lenders may stipulate that specific milestones be met before releasing further loan tranches.
- ○ **Exit Strategy Proof:** Some lenders may want evidence of a solid exit strategy, such as a confirmed buyer, refinancing agreement, or marketable property value increase post-renovation.
- ○ **Additional guarantees:** Some lenders may require additional guarantees to mitigate their risk. These could include personal guarantees from the borrower, cross-collateralization of other properties, or corporate guarantees for company borrowers.

Understanding these terms thoroughly and preparing for potential additional requirements can help you secure a bridging loan that aligns with your investment goals and minimize unexpected challenges during the loan term.

6.3 How to Secure the Best Rates and Terms

Securing the best possible rates and terms on a bridging loan depends on several factors, including your financial profile, the lender's risk appetite, and the project's potential.

Here are a few tips to help you secure favourable terms:

- **Build a Strong Application:** Lenders assess risk based on the strength of your application. Be sure to provide detailed information about your project, including a clear exit strategy, accurate property valuations, and your experience as an investor. A well-prepared application with detailed financials and a realistic timeline will make you a more attractive borrower.

  In doing so, be transparent and do not hide information. Lenders have a variety of sources to cross validate the information you supply. For example, inflating the value of your assets of the gross development value (GDV) of your project will make you look unprofessional and unreliable. In addition, reusing material you have prepared for other lenders might save you time but will reduce your chances of securing a loan since your new lender will assume you have been rejected elsewhere and will scrutinise you more closely.

- **Negotiate Fees**: While interest rates may be nonnegotiable, some fees are flexible. Discuss the possibility of reducing arrangement fees or waiving exit fees, especially if you have a strong credit history or are a repeat borrower. For instance, at Integer Investments, we have special deals for returning clients with a solid track record or with high credit scores.
- **Improve Your Credit Profile**: Lenders may offer lower interest rates and higher LTVs to borrowers with strong credit scores. If you have any outstanding credit issues, resolve them before applying for a bridging loan to increase your chances of securing better terms.
- **Offer Additional Security**: In some cases, offering additional security (such as another property) can help reduce the risk for the lender, which may result in lower interest rates or more favourable terms. However, this strategy also increases your personal financial exposure, so it should be considered carefully.
- **Establish Relationships with Lenders**: Building a strong relationship with a lender can lead to better deals on future projects. Shopping around can save you costs in the short term, but having a solid relationship with a lender might be more beneficial in the long term. For example, returning clients at Integer Investments often benefit from lower fees and quicker approvals, as we've built trust and understand their investment strategies.

Conclusion: Choosing the Right Lender for Your Project

Selecting the right lender is one of the most important decisions you'll make when using bridging finance. The terms and conditions of your loan will have a direct impact on your project's profitability, so it's essential to do thorough research, compare lenders, and negotiate where possible. By focusing on reputable lenders with transparent terms and a strong track record, you'll be well positioned to secure financing that supports your investment goals.

In the next chapter, we will delve into advanced strategies for property investors using bridging finance, exploring how you can maximize returns and leverage short-term loans for long-term success.

CHAPTER 7

Legal and Regulatory Aspects of Bridging Loans in the UK—A Summary of the Legal Aspects

(By Carlos Torres)

Note: This chapter provides only a brief summary of certain aspects of secured lending and should not be considered legal advice. It is for general informational purposes only. Additionally, terms commonly used in practice have been included in this guide, but their meanings may vary depending on the legal and commercial context. Always seek professional legal advice for specific transactions.

Bridging finance can be a powerful tool for property investors, but it's essential to navigate the legal and regulatory framework to ensure compliance and protect yourself from potential risks. In this chapter, we'll explore the key legal aspects of bridging loans, including the role of the Financial Conduct Authority (FCA), the legal documentation involved, and important regulations that investors need to consider when taking out a bridging loan. It is important that you consult with a legal professional to avoid unnecessary legal risks. This chapter is not intended to be a comprehensive legal review.

7.1 FCA Regulations on Bridging Loans

In the UK, bridging loans can fall into two categories: **regulated** and **unregulated** loans. One of the key distinctions is whether the loan is used to purchase or refinance a borrower's primary residence.

- **Regulated bridging loans** are overseen by the **Financial Conduct Authority (FCA)**. These loans are typically taken out by individuals borrowing against their own home or a property intended as their primary residence. The FCA provides consumer protections to ensure that borrowers understand the terms of the loan and can afford to repay it. Lenders must follow stringent guidelines, including affordability checks and ensuring that loan agreements are transparent.
- **Unregulated bridging loans**, on the other hand, are not overseen by the FCA and are used primarily for investment purposes. These loans are more common in property development or investment projects, such as house flipping, auction purchases, or commercial property acquisitions. Investors should be aware that, while unregulated loans offer greater flexibility, they do not benefit from the same protections as regulated loans.

Most bridging lenders specialise in **unregulated bridging loans** tailored to property investors. However, it is important that they ensure full transparency in loan agreements, providing clients with clear terms and conditions to avoid any misunderstandings.

Secured Lending

Bridge loans are a form of secured lending. Secured lending represents a financial arrangement in which a borrower offers an asset—known as collateral—to the lender as security for a loan. If the borrower cannot meet their repayment obligations, the lender is legally entitled to take possession of the collateral to recover the outstanding debt. This collateral often includes significant assets such as land, vehicles, or other property of value, ensuring the lender's risk is mitigated by the ability to reclaim and potentially sell the asset.

The legal framework governing secured lending in the UK is robust, designed to protect the interests of both lenders and borrowers. Central to this framework is the concept of enforceable security interests, which give lenders a legal claim over the offered assets. These security interests are formalised through documentation such as legal charges, mortgages, or debentures—depending on the nature of the loan and the asset involved.

The decision to enter into secured lending arrangements has significant legal implications. While access to funds may be facilitated at more favourable terms due to reduced risk for lenders, borrowers must be aware of their risk of losing the security.

In the context of bridging loans, which often involve tight repayment schedules, the secured nature of these loans is a defining characteristic. Borrowers must understand not only the advantages of leveraging assets for immediate financing, but also the legal responsibilities and potential consequences of such agreements.

7.2 Legal Mortgages Over Property

A legal mortgage is one of the most common forms of security used in secured lending. It is a legal mechanism that grants a lender an interest in the borrower's property as security for a loan, while the borrower retains ownership of the property. This arrangement provides lenders with significant protections: if the borrower defaults on their repayment obligations, the lender has the right to enforce the mortgage and seek repayment through the sale of the property.

Legal mortgages are formalised through a deed, which outlines the terms of the loan, the rights and obligations of both parties, and the consequences of default. For property transactions in the UK, these agreements must be registered with HM Land Registry to ensure their enforceability and to provide public notice of the lender's interest in the property.

Often, the amount secured by the legal mortgage is not limited to the amount the borrower borrows against the Property. The agreement may, in fact, cover all monies and liabilities owed by the borrower to the lender at any time, whether these liabilities exist at a certain time or are incurred in the future and whether or not any such liability is contingent upon the occurrence of some other event.

The legal mortgage over land will certainly include several key clauses to protect the lender's interests.

In the *representations and warranties* clause, the borrower will be confirming to the lender that some matters have not occurred and will not occur during the term of the loan, such as:

- It is not insolvent.
- Any guarantor is not bankrupt or at risk of being made bankrupt.
- No event of default (as defined in the agreement between lender and borrower) is continuing or would be expected to result from the making of the loan.
- There are no litigation arbitration or administrative proceedings of or before any court arbitral body or agency that if adversely determined would reasonably be expected to have an adverse effect on the Borrower's ability to comply with its obligations under the facility agreement with the lender.
- It will use the property in compliance with laws, maintain consents, and promptly address any legal requirements related to the property.
- It will not create further encumbrances or dispose of any part of the property without prior written consent from the lender.

In the *property covenants* clause, there will be many provisions requiring the borrower to comply to many matters, such as:

- To keep the property, including fixtures and fittings, in good condition and promptly replace any worn-out fixtures.
- Not to alter the property without the lender's consent.
- Not to undertake planning, development, or change the property's use without prior lender's consent.
- To insure the property for its full reinstatement value, with the lender's interest being noted in the insurance policy.
- Not to grant leases, tenancies, or sharing possession without lender's consent.
- To adhere to existing covenants, stipulations, and conditions affecting the property.

Common clauses include the **charging clause**, which formally creates the security interest over the property in favor of the lender. The

covenant to repay requires the borrower to repay the loan in accordance with the agreed terms. An **insurance clause** mandates that the property must be adequately insured, with the lender named as an interested party. The **maintenance and repair clause** obligates the borrower to keep the property in good condition. A **default and enforcement clause** outlines the lender's rights in case of nonpayment, including the ability to take possession or sell the property. Additionally, a **negative pledge clause** may restrict the borrower from granting further charges over the property without the lender's consent. These provisions collectively ensure that the lender's security is maintained and enforceable.

7.3 First- and Second-Ranking Legal Mortgages over Property

One critical aspect of a legal mortgage is its priority status, which is established based on the order of registration. This priority determines the lender's rights relative to other creditors of the borrower, particularly important in the event of a borrower's financial distress.

First-Ranking Legal Mortgage over Land:

A first legal charge represents the primary security interest over a property. The lender holding the first charge has the first right to repayment from the proceeds of a property's sale if the borrower defaults. Typically, a first legal charge is used for major loans, such as standard residential or commercial mortgages, where the lender provides the bulk of the financing required to acquire the property.

The lender with the first-charge benefits from the highest level of security, as their claim will be satisfied before any other creditors. This often allows them to offer lower interest rates and more favorable loan terms since they face less risk.

Second-Ranking Legal Mortgage over Land:

A second legal charge is a subordinate security interest placed on a property. This charge is only enforceable after the first charge is satisfied.

Borrowers often use second charges to access additional funding while already having a first charge in place.

Second charges inherently carry more risk for lenders, as they are dependent on the remaining equity in the property after the first charge has been repaid. Consequently, loans secured by second charges often feature higher interest rates and stricter terms. Lenders will also carefully assess the property's remaining equity and the borrower's financial standing before agreeing to a second charge.

From the borrower's perspective, the ability to secure a second charge provides flexibility but also introduces additional financial commitments and risks. For both lenders and borrowers, it is crucial to clearly understand the priority structure and implications of holding or granting first and second legal charges.

Additional legal charges, such as third ranking or beyond, can be taken. However, in most cases, lenders primarily secure first and second legal charges.

7.4 Protecting the Lender: The Due Diligence Process

To safeguard their financial interests, lenders undertake a rigorous due diligence process before advancing funds under a secured loan. This process ensures that the property used as security not only holds sufficient equity but also carries no legal risks that could compromise its value. The property due diligence process is essential to evaluate the lender's ability to recover the loan if the borrower defaults.

It is worth noting that the "UK Finance Mortgage Lenders' Handbook" contains a set of guidelines and best practices for financial institutions in the UK. The Handbook is published by **UK Finance** and provides regulatory guidance, industry standards, and practical advice on topics like mortgages, lending, fraud prevention, compliance, and risk management.

It is commonly used by lenders, solicitors, and conveyancers, particularly in relation to mortgage lending practices and legal requirements.

Breakdown of the Due Diligence:

1. Title Checks
A fundamental aspect of due diligence involves verifying the property's legal title. This ensures, in particular, that:

- The borrower holds legal ownership of the property.
- There are no restrictions, easements, or covenants that may affect its value or marketability.

Lenders rely on solicitors to review the property's title register at HM Land Registry and ensure the title is unencumbered, apart from any disclosed interests.

2. Property Searches
Property searches are conducted to uncover any potential risks associated with the property. The specific searches required will be determined based on factors such as the property's geographical area, historical use, and any known issues that could affect its value or suitability as security for the loan.
The most commonly commissioned searches include:

- Local Authority Search
  This search identifies planning permissions, building regulations compliance, or pending enforcement actions. It also reveals any compulsory purchase orders or road schemes that may impact the property's value or usability.
- Environmental Search
  An environmental search assesses whether the property is at risk of contamination or located in areas prone to flooding or subsidence. These issues could significantly impact the property's value or render it unsuitable for use.
- Chancel Repair Liability Search
  Chancel repair liability checks determine whether the property owner may be legally required to contribute to the upkeep of a local parish church. While less common, this liability can still pose unexpected financial burdens.

- Water and Drainage Search
This search confirms the property's connection to public water and sewerage systems. It also identifies whether any water mains or drainage infrastructure run through the property, which could restrict future development.
- Coal and Mining Search
Particularly relevant in former mining areas, this search reveals whether the property is affected by past mining activities. Risks such as ground instability or subsidence could severely impact both safety and value.

In certain circumstances, lenders may agree to proceed without requiring standard property searches. However, in such cases, the lender will typically require a "non-search" indemnity policy to protect its interests against potential risks that the missing searches might have revealed. This policy provides financial coverage in the event of any adverse issues arising, such as undisclosed restrictions, planning breaches, or environmental concerns. The decision to proceed without searches and rely on an indemnity policy is subject to the lender's discretion and must align with its risk assessment and lending criteria.

3. Occupational Rights

Assessing the occupation of the property is also important. The lender will be interested in establishing whether the property is owner-occupied, tenanted, or vacant. If the property is occupied by a third party, details of their rights will be investigated.

If tenants occupy the property, the lender's solicitor will review any occupational agreements, noting, in particular:

- Rent amount
- Term and renewal rights
- Tenant obligations and restrictions
- Any break clauses or forfeiture provisions
- Matrimonial rights
- Compliance with regulations (such as whether the Prescribed Information has been provided to tenants under assured shorthold tenancies (ASTs))

○ Protected Tenancies: Under the Landlord and Tenant Act 1954 (LTA54), commercial tenants may have security of tenure, making it difficult for a lender to recover possession in case of default by the borrower.

Lenders will often request confirmation from the borrower and solicitors regarding occupation status. If necessary, they may insist on vacant possession or require rental income to be assigned to them as additional security.

4. Borrower Due Diligence

In addition to the property investigation and checks, lenders ought to evaluate the borrower's financial stability and legal standing. Borrower due diligence typically includes the following:

- Insolvency Register Check: This search ensures that the borrower is not subject to bankruptcy proceedings or other insolvency-related actions. Lending to a borrower who is insolvent or under a voluntary arrangement could expose the lender to significant risks.
- Identity Verification: Anti-money laundering (AML) regulations require lenders to verify the borrower's identity. This includes obtaining and reviewing identification documents and proof of address.
- Existing Charges Review: An examination of existing charges registered against the borrower's property ensures there is sufficient equity to support the proposed loan.
- Companies House: A search at Companies House ensures the borrower is an active entity. The lender's solicitor will review the company's constitutional documents, including its articles of association, and filing history, to verify the company's authority to borrow and grant security. The search will also confirm that the directors and officers signing the loan documents have the necessary authority to bind the company.

7.5 Other Common Forms of Security

In addition to securing a loan against property, lenders may require additional forms of security to further protect their interests. These securities provide extra assurances, particularly in complex transactions or when the primary collateral alone may not fully cover the loan's risk.

1. Debenture

A debenture is perhaps the most frequently used security instrument in corporate lending. It provides the lender with a charge over the borrower's assets, which can include tangible and intangible assets such as equipment, inventory, receivables, and intellectual property.

Debentures may be structured as:

- **Fixed Charge**: Secured against specific assets, such as machinery or real estate, preventing the borrower from selling or otherwise disposing of the asset without the lender's consent.
- **Floating Charge**: Secured against general assets or categories of assets, such as inventory or accounts receivable, allowing the borrower to manage and trade these assets in the ordinary course of business.

In the event of default, the lender can appoint a receiver or initiate enforcement proceedings under the debenture to recover outstanding debts.

It is important you understand that in the event of default of the loan by the borrower, the lender will be able to enforce its security over all of the specified company assets, and, as mentioned earlier, not just the company's property or buildings. The lender can also enforce security against, among others, the company's debt, cash, and work in progress, all of which are fluid and get "crystallised" (i.e., fixed in value) on the date of the appointment of a receiver or administrator.

The debenture will be registered at Companies House as a charge over the company and its assets. Once registered, the debenture will become publicly available to download by third parties. In practice, this means that any potential future lender will be able to view the relevant agreement. Borrowers should be aware that often they are responsible to ensure that the charge is removed or "discharged" from the Companies House register as soon as the loan is redeemed, as this process of discharging the Companies House's charge may be overlooked by the parties, which may impact or delay future borrowing.

2. Personal Guarantee

A personal guarantee is a commitment made by an individual—often a director, shareholder, or other principal of the borrowing entity—to personally repay the loan if the borrower defaults. This security is particularly common in situations where the borrower is a limited company with limited liability, adding an additional layer of resource to the lender in respect to the company's obligations.

By providing a personal guarantee, the guarantor assumes significant risk, putting personal assets such as savings, investments, or even their home at stake. For lenders, it acts as a powerful incentive for the guarantor to ensure the borrower meets its obligations.

Independent Legal Advice (ILA): When personal guarantees are involved, lenders often require borrowers to seek ILA to ensure that the borrower fully understands the implications of their commitment. The ILA has several purposes:

- **Understanding Obligations**: The solicitor providing the advice explains to the borrower what the personal guarantee is, ensuring that the borrower fully understands their personal liability, including the risks of repayment shortfalls or default scenarios.
- **Ensuring Voluntary Agreement**: The ILA confirms that the borrower is willingly entering into the agreement and is not under undue influence.
- **Protecting Both Parties**: Lenders request ILA as a safeguard against potential disputes. If a borrower later claims they did not understand the terms of the personal guarantee, the ILA serves as proof that the terms were clearly explained.
- **Detailed Process**: During the ILA process, the borrower will meet with an independent solicitor (not associated with the lender) to review the documentation. This solicitor will explain the legal and financial implications in detail and ensure that the borrower has no questions or concerns before entering into the personal guarantee with the lender.
- **Certification**: After the ILA meeting, the solicitor will typically provide a certificate confirming that the borrower has received the independent advice and fully understands their obligations.

The ILA process can add a step to the overall timeline, so borrowers should plan accordingly and engage an experienced solicitor early to avoid delays.

3. Corporate Guarantee

A corporate guarantee operates similar to a personal guarantee but is provided by another company—often a parent company or affiliate entity—on behalf of the borrower. This security ensures that the guaranteeing company will step in to repay the loan if the borrower defaults.

Corporate guarantees are frequently used in group structures where the borrowing entity may be a subsidiary with limited assets.

Combining Security Instruments:
Lenders often combine these forms of security to create a robust safety net. For instance, in a typical secured loan transaction, the lender might hold:

- A **first legal charge** over the borrower's property.
- A **debenture** securing the borrower's business assets.
- A **personal guarantee** from the directors of the borrowing entity (with ILA).

This layered approach ensures that, in the event of default, the lender has multiple avenues for recovery, reducing the risk of financial loss.

For borrowers, offering additional security such as guarantees or debentures can improve their borrowing terms, but it also increases their exposure. It is critical for borrowers to carefully weigh the risks against the benefits.

7.6 Some of the Consequences of Default

When a borrower defaults on a loan, the lender has the legal right to enforce its security to recover the outstanding debt. The specific course of action depends on the type of security held by the lender. In the following, we outline the consequences of default and enforcement measures available in cases where the lender has a legal charge against property, a debenture, and a personal guarantee.

1. Enforcement Against Property

If the lender holds a legal charge against the borrower's property (whether as a first or second charge), it has the right to:

- **Take Possession**: The lender can initiate proceedings to take physical possession of the property.
- **Force a Sale**: Following possession, the lender can sell the property to recover the outstanding debt. The proceeds of the sale are applied to the loan balance, with any surplus returned to the borrower, provided there are no subordinate creditors with claims.

If the property's value is insufficient to cover the debt, the lender may turn to other securities, such as debentures or personal guarantees, to recover the shortfall.

2. Enforcement of a Debenture

As previously mentioned, a debenture provides lenders with security over a range of the borrower's assets, and its enforcement typically involves the following steps:

- **Appointment of a Receiver**: Under the terms of the debenture, the lender can appoint an administrative receiver to take control of the borrower's business and sell its assets to repay the debt.
- **Seizure and Sale of Assets**: Assets covered by the debenture, such as machinery, stock, or receivables, can be seized and sold to recover the loan.
- **Insolvency Proceedings**: If enforcement measures are insufficient to recover the debt, the lender may petition for the borrower's liquidation.

3. Enforcement of a Personal Guarantee

When a personal guarantee is in place, the lender can pursue the guarantor directly for the unpaid debt. The most common steps are:

- **Demand for Payment**: The lender formally demands payment from the guarantor in accordance with the guarantee's terms.
- **Legal Proceedings**: If the guarantor fails to pay, the lender may initiate legal action to enforce the guarantee, which could result in a court order for repayment.
- **Attachment of Personal Assets**: Once a judgment is obtained, the lender can seek to recover the debt through enforcement measures such as charging orders, or the sale of the guarantor's assets.

Practical Implications
The lender's ability to pursue multiple securities allows it to recover debts efficiently while minimizing financial loss. However, this approach can have significant consequences for borrowers and guarantors:

- **For Borrowers**: The loss of property, disruption to business operations, and potential insolvency.
- **For Guarantors**: Financial liability that could extend to personal bankruptcy or the sale of personal assets.

Borrowers and guarantors must fully understand the terms of their agreements, as well as the potential repercussions of default. Lenders, in turn, must adhere to legal and procedural requirements during enforcement to avoid challenges or claims of unfair treatment

7.7 Key Legal Considerations for Investors

When using bridging finance, investors must take several legal considerations into account to ensure their project runs smoothly:

- **Understanding the Legal Timeline**: Property transactions, particularly those involving bridging loans, often have strict deadlines. In an auction scenario, for example, completion is typically required within 28 days. Ensuring that the legal process aligns with these deadlines is essential to avoid penalties or missed opportunities. Delays in obtaining a bridging loan can result in legal complications, such as losing a property deposit or being sued for breach of contract.

- **Extension Terms**: Many bridging loans are taken out for short periods (4 to 12 months), with the understanding that the loan will be repaid through refinancing or selling the property. However, if the project is delayed, it's crucial to understand the terms for extending the loan. Some lenders charge **extension fees**, which can add significantly to the project's costs. Before taking out a loan, investors should have a clear understanding of these fees and whether they can negotiate more favourable terms.

- **Planning Permissions and Legal Restrictions**: In some development projects, investors may require planning permission before proceeding with renovations or conversions. If the project involves significant changes, such as converting a property into an HMO (house in multiple occupation), investors must ensure they have the correct permissions in place. Delays in obtaining planning approval can cause legal complications, particularly if the bridging loan is contingent upon specific development milestones being met.

Lenders should work with experienced legal teams to ensure that the legal aspects of their loan arrangements are handled smoothly, assisting investors to avoid potential delays and penalties. Some lenders recommend using only one set of solicitors for both the lender and the borrower since the loan documents are non-negotiable. Having one set of solicitors not only reduces costs to the borrower but also avoids delays. Solicitors are generally busy professionals and communication between two legal firms (in addition to the sellers' solicitors) can add weeks to the closing timeline.

Conclusion: Navigating the Legal Landscape of Bridging Finance

Understanding the legal and regulatory framework of bridging loans is essential for property investors to ensure their projects run smoothly and within the bounds of the law. While unregulated loans offer more flexibility, they come with increased risk and responsibility. Engaging experienced legal professionals and ensuring that all documentation is clear and transparent are key steps in securing successful bridging finance.

The next chapter will explore how to choose the right bridging finance lender and evaluate the different options available in the UK market to ensure the best possible terms for your investment projects.

CHAPTER 8

Tax and Accounting Considerations

Navigating the tax landscape is crucial for property investors utilizing bridging finance. This chapter delves into key tax considerations, including stamp duty land tax (SDLT), capital gains tax (CGT), the offsetting of bridging interest, and the potential use of special purpose vehicles (SPVs). However, make sure you discuss this with a professional as rules and regulations change regularly.

8.1 Tax Implications and Accounting Best Practices

Tax planning is a critical component of any property investment strategy, and bridging finance introduces specific tax implications that investors need to manage carefully. Being aware of these tax considerations can help investors avoid unnecessary liabilities and ensure that their profits are maximized. This section is not supposed to be an exhaustive list, and investors should work with an accountant to optimize their tax exposure.

Tax-Deductible Interest: One of the advantages of using bridging finance is that the interest paid on loans for investment purposes is typically tax deductible. If the property is being used for rental income or will be sold at a profit, the interest on the bridging loan can be deducted from taxable profits. This is a significant benefit for investors, as it can offset the higher interest rates associated with bridging finance.

For example, if an investor pays £10,000 in interest on a bridging loan while renovating a property, they can deduct this expense when calculating their taxable profit from the eventual sale or rental income, thereby reducing their overall tax burden, proportionally to their tax rate. For example, if the tax rate is 25 percent, the actual cost of the interests will be £7,500 as there will be £2,500 in tax savings.

CGT: Investors should also be aware of CGT, which applies when selling a property for a profit. Careful tax planning can help minimize CGT liabilities. For instance, holding a property for a longer period may reduce the CGT rate or reinvesting the proceeds into other qualifying assets can defer or reduce the tax owed.

SDLT: In addition to CGT, investors using bridging finance should factor in SDLT on property acquisitions. In certain cases, investors may be eligible for SDLT relief, particularly if the property is purchased for development or conversion (more details follow). Various free online sources offer stamp duty calculators. In recent years, the UK government has increased the stamp duty for investors owning more than one property.

Value-Added Tax (VAT) for Commercial and Mixed-Use Projects: For larger developments, especially those involving commercial or mixed-use properties, investors may also need to consider **VAT**. Developers may be able to reclaim VAT on construction expenses, but this requires careful planning and compliance with HMRC (His Majesty's Revenue and Customs) regulations.

Best Tax and Accounting Practices:
- **Detailed Record-Keeping**: Maintain accurate and detailed records of all project costs, including loan interest, fees, development expenses, and professional services. This ensures that all deductible expenses are captured and helps avoid discrepancies during tax filing.
- **Work with a Specialist Accountant**: Engaging an accountant who specializes in property investments is essential for ensuring compliance with tax laws and maximizing tax efficiency. They can help manage your tax strategy and keep you informed of any changes in regulations that could affect your investments. A firm Integer Investments likes working with is Thompson Accountancy Services in Sunderland.
- **Exit Strategy Tax Planning**: Plan your exit strategy with tax implications in mind, whether through selling or refinancing. Understanding the tax consequences of each option will allow you to choose the most advantageous route for your investment.

Conclusion: Maximizing Returns with Advanced Strategies

Bridging finance, when used strategically, can be an invaluable tool for property investors looking to accelerate growth, take advantage of large-scale development opportunities, and optimize their tax positions. Whether it's leveraging staged financing for complex developments, rapidly expanding a property portfolio through efficient capital recycling, or carefully managing tax liabilities, bridging loans offer flexibility and potential for significant returns. By understanding and applying these advanced strategies, investors can unlock the full potential of their property investments.

8.2 Stamp Duty Land Tax

Overview: Stamp duty land tax is a tax levied on property purchases in England and Northern Ireland. The amount payable depends on the property's purchase price and the buyer's circumstances, such as first-time buyer status or the acquisition of additional properties.

Recent Changes: As of October 31, 2024, significant changes have been implemented:

- **Additional Property Surcharge:** The surcharge for purchasing additional residential properties (e.g., second homes or buy-to-let investments) has increased from 3 to 5 percent.
- **Standard Rates:** The general SDLT threshold will revert to £125,000 from April 2025, down from the temporary £250,000 threshold (source: www.gov.uk).

Current SDLT Rates (Effective October 31, 2024):
- **Standard Residential Purchases:**
  - Up to £250,000: 0 percent
  - £250,001 to £925,000: 5 percent
  - £925,001 to £1.5 million: 10 percent
  - Above £1.5 million: 12 percent
- **Additional Properties (Including 5 Percent Surcharge):**
  - Up to £250,000: 5 percent
  - £250,001 to £925,000: 10 percent

- £925,001 to £1.5 million: 15 percent
- Above £1.5 million: 17 percent

Example Calculation: If you purchase a buy-to-let property for £400,000:

- First £250,000 at 5 percent: £12,500
- Next £150,000 at 10 percent: £15,000
- **Total** SDLT: £27,500

If you're not present in the UK for at least 183 days (6 months) during the 12 months before your purchase, you are "not a UK resident" for the purposes of SDLT. You'll usually pay a 2 percent surcharge if you're buying a residential property in England or Northern Ireland.

Planning Tips:
- **Transaction Timing:** Completing purchases before April 2025 can result in SDLT savings due to current thresholds.
- Multiple Dwellings Relief (MDR): If buying multiple properties in a single transaction, MDR may reduce the SDLT liability.

Stamp duty land tax (SDLT) is a significant consideration for property buyers in England and Northern Ireland. However, under certain circumstances, you may be eligible for a refund on overpaid SDLT. Here's an overview of key scenarios where refunds may apply:

1. **Multiple Dwellings Relief**
   If you've purchased multiple dwellings in a single transaction or a series of linked transactions, you might qualify for MDR, which can reduce your SDLT liability. If MDR wasn't claimed during the initial SDLT return, or if there was a miscalculation, you could be entitled to a refund.
   Example:
   Sam purchased a property comprising two dwellings for £995,000. Without MDR, he paid £40,750 in SDLT. By claiming MDR, his SDLT liability reduced, resulting in a refund of £16,000.

2. **Refund on Additional 3 Percent Surcharge for Second Homes**
   If you paid the additional 3 percent SDLT surcharge on a new property purchase, intending it to be your main residence, and sold your previous main residence within three years, you're eligible to claim a refund of the surcharge.
   Example:
       Nick bought a second property for £275,000, paying an additional 3 percent surcharge. After selling his previous main residence within the allowable period, he became eligible for a refund of £8,250.

3. **Uninhabitable Properties**
   Purchasing a property deemed uninhabitable may qualify one for non-residential SDLT rates, which are lower than residential rates. If you initially paid the higher residential rate, you might be entitled to a refund of the difference.

4. **Properties with Annexes**
   Properties with self-contained annexes may qualify for MDR, potentially reducing SDLT liability. If this relief wasn't applied during the initial transaction, a refund might be possible.

5. **Group Relief**
   Transfers of property between companies within the same group can be exempt from SDLT under group relief provisions. If SDLT was paid on such a transaction, a refund may be due.

Claiming a Refund:
- **Time Limits:** Generally, you have 12 months from the filing date of the original SDLT return to amend it and claim a refund. In certain circumstances, this period may extend up to 36 months.
- **Documentation:** Maintain thorough records, including contracts, proof of property status, and evidence of sale of previous residences, to support your refund claim.
- **Professional Assistance:** Given the complexities involved in SDLT regulations and reliefs, consulting with a property tax specialist is advisable to ensure compliance and optimize potential refunds.

8.3 Capital Gains Tax

Overview: Capital gains tax is charged on the profit made from selling a property that isn't your primary residence. The rate depends on your taxable income and the type of asset sold. Losses from other disposals can be offset against gains to reduce your CGT liability.

Recent Changes: Effective October 31, 2024, CGT rates have increased:

- **Non-residential Property and Other Assets**
  - Basic-Rate Taxpayers: Increased from 10 to 18 percent
  - Higher-Rate Taxpayers: Increased from 20 to 24 percent
- **Residential Property**
  Rates remain at 18 percent for basic-rate taxpayers and 24 percent for higher-rate taxpayers. (www.gov.uk/guidance/capital-gains-tax-rates-and-allowances)

Annual Exempt Amount: For the 2024–2025 tax year, the CGT allowance is £3,000. Gains above this amount are subject to CGT. (www.gov.uk/guidance/capital-gains-tax-rates-and-allowances)

Example Calculation: If you're a higher-rate taxpayer and sell a residential investment property with a gain of £50,000:

- Deduct Annual Exempt Amount: £50,000 − £3,000 = £47,000
- CGT at 24 percent: £47,000 × 24 percent = £11,280

Planning Tips:
- **Utilize Allowances:** Consider spreading disposals over multiple tax years to maximize annual exemptions.
- **Ownership Structure:** Joint ownership with a spouse can double the CGT allowance.

8.4 Offset of Bridging Interest for Investment Properties

Overview: Interest paid on bridging loans for investment properties is generally tax deductible, reducing your taxable rental income or capital gains.

Key Considerations:
- **Allowable Deductions:** Interest is deductible if the loan is used for property acquisition, refurbishment, or enhancement intended for rental or resale.
- **Proper Documentation:** Maintain detailed records of interest payments and ensure the loan's purpose aligns with investment activities.

Example: If you incur £10,000 in bridging loan interest for refurbishing a rental property, this amount can be deducted from your rental income, reducing your income tax liability.

Planning Tips:
- **Consult a Tax Professional:** Ensure compliance with HMRC regulations and optimize tax benefits.
- **Accurate Record-Keeping:** Keep all loan agreements and interest statements for tax reporting.

8.5 Use of a Special Purpose Vehicle

What Is a Special Purpose Vehicle?
A special purpose vehicle (SPV) is a limited company established solely for owning and managing specific assets or projects. In the context of property investment, an SPV is commonly used to acquire, hold, and manage property portfolios or individual investments. The main purpose of an SPV is to isolate financial risks and optimize tax and operational efficiencies.

Advantages of Using an SPV in Property Investment:
1. **Tax Efficiency**
   - **Corporation Tax Benefits:** Special purpose vehicles are subject to corporation tax on rental income and profits, which is generally lower than personal income tax rates, especially for higher-rate taxpayers.
   - **Deductibility of Expenses:** Mortgage interest and other property-related expenses are fully deductible for corporation tax

purposes, unlike personal ownership, where interest deductions
are restricted.

- ○ **Capital Gains Tax (CGT):** When selling properties, SPVs may
offer more flexibility in offsetting gains against company losses
or reinvesting profits into other projects without immediate tax
liabilities.

2. **Limited Liability**
   - ○ An SPV limits personal liability for debts or legal claims related
   to the property investment, as the liability is confined to the
   company.

3. **Streamlined Ownership Structure**
   - ○ Multiple investors can pool resources and share ownership of the
   SPV through company shares, simplifying the distribution of
   profits and decision-making processes.

4. **Ease of Transfer**
   - ○ Transferring ownership of a property held in an SPV can be
   achieved by selling company shares rather than transferring the
   property itself, potentially reducing stamp duty and legal costs.

5. **Professional Financing Options**
   - ○ Lenders may offer favourable terms for SPVs, particularly for
   buy-to-let or bridging finance, as the entity is seen as a business
   rather than an individual borrower.

Considerations When Using an SPV:

1. **Setup Costs and Administration**
   - ○ Setting up an SPV involves incorporation fees and ongoing administrative requirements, such as annual filings, accounting,
   and corporate tax returns.

2. **Mortgage Accessibility**
   - ○ Not all lenders offer mortgages to SPVs, and interest rates may
   be slightly higher than those offered to individuals. However,
   this gap has been narrowing as SPVs become more common in
   property investment.

3. **Tax Implications**
   - ○ While SPVs can be tax efficient, they are not universally beneficial. For smaller portfolios or properties intended for personal

use, individual ownership may be more advantageous. Professional tax advice is essential to determine the best structure.

4. **Exit Strategy**
   - Selling shares in an SPV to transfer property ownership may trigger different tax consequences, such as stamp duty land tax (SDLT) or corporation tax on capital gains. Proper planning is crucial to mitigate these liabilities.

Steps to Establish an SPV for Property Investment:

1. **Incorporate the SPV**
   - Register the company with Companies House, choosing an appropriate name and designating its purpose (e.g., "property management").
   - Appoint directors and shareholders.

2. **Define the Business Activity**
   - Clearly state the company's focus in the Articles of Association. For property investments, this could include "acquisition and management of real estate assets."

3. **Open a Business Bank Account**
   - Use a dedicated business account for all transactions related to the SPV, ensuring clear financial separation from personal finances.

4. **Arrange Financing**
   - Work with lenders that specialize in SPV mortgages or bridging loans. Present a strong business case, including rental yield projections and an exit strategy.

5. **Ensure Compliance**
   - File annual accounts, maintain accurate records, and comply with corporate tax obligations to avoid penalties.

Best Practices for Using an SPV:

- **Seek Professional Advice:** Consult accountants and solicitors experienced in property investments and corporate structures to ensure the SPV is tailored to your specific needs.
- **Plan Long-Term:** Consider your growth strategy, tax implications, and exit plans before setting up an SPV.

- **Stay Compliant:** Regularly update filings and maintain clear records to avoid legal or financial issues.

By utilizing an SPV strategically, property investors can enjoy enhanced tax efficiency, reduced liability, and streamlined operations, making it a valuable tool for managing property investments effectively.

Conclusion

Understanding and planning for tax and accounting implications is crucial for maximizing returns and ensuring compliance in property investments. Bridging finance, when strategically paired with careful tax planning, can unlock significant opportunities for investors. Whether it's leveraging allowable deductions, structuring transactions to minimize taxes, or exploring the benefits of SPVs, professional guidance is key to optimizing your investment outcomes.

By staying informed about the latest tax regulations and tailoring strategies to individual circumstances, investors can mitigate financial risks and enhance profitability. Always consult a qualified tax adviser to navigate these complexities and ensure your property investments remain both lucrative and compliant.

CHAPTER 9

Practical "How-To" Guides

9.1 How to Buy at Auction with Bridging Finance

Step-by-Step Guide

1. **Research Auctions and Properties**
   - Identify reputable auction houses and study their catalogues. The UK hosts several prominent real estate auction houses that facilitate the buying and selling of residential and commercial properties. Here are some of the main auction houses:
     1. **Auction House UK**: Recognized as the UK's largest residential and commercial property auction company, Auction House UK operates numerous auction rooms nationwide and conducts regular national online auctions. (www.auctionhouse.co.uk/home)
     2. **Savills Auctions**: With over 20 years of auction experience, Savills offers a wide selection of residential and commercial properties. They provide comprehensive services for both buyers and sellers. (https://auctions.savills.co.uk)
     3. **Allsop**: As one of the UK's leading property consultancies, Allsop holds regular auctions featuring a diverse range of properties across the country. (www.allsop.co.uk/auctions/residential-auctions)
   - Focus on properties with high potential for value addition, such as those requiring refurbishment or in areas with strong rental demand.
   - Review the legal pack for each property, paying close attention to title issues, planning permissions, or restrictive covenants. This process might be time-consuming, and requiring investment of time even if you do not end up buying the property. Further, check for other conditions such as fees, buyer's

premium, property access, payment requirements. Some of these extra conditions can be onerous.

2. **Prepare Your Finances**
   - **Secure a Decision in Principle (DIP)**

     Obtain a decision in principle from a bridging lender before attending the auction. This ensures that you have access to funds quickly once you secure a property. Be thorough when providing the necessary information to the lender and ensure the offer is reliable. This minimizes the risk of the lender withdrawing after you've committed to purchasing the property and paid the 10 percent deposit, which is non-refunded if you fail to complete the purchase. However, make sure that the price you pay for the property is in line with market values. If the lender's valuation is lower than your final bid, the offer might be rescinded leaving you without finance.

   - **Set Your Maximum Bid**

     Calculate your maximum bid carefully, factoring in all associated costs such as stamp duty, auction fees, and refurbishment expenses. Be realistic about your budget and avoid the temptation to exceed your limit on auction day, as this can lead to financial strain or project overruns.

3. **Attend the Auction (or Bid Online)**
   - Stick to your budget and avoid emotional bidding.
   - Once you win, pay the required deposit (usually 10 percent of the purchase price) immediately to secure the property.

4. **Complete the Transaction**
   - Work with a solicitor to finalize the purchase within the auction deadline (typically 28 days, but 56 days can be negotiated in some cases).
   - Ensure the bridging loan is ready for drawdown to meet the auction's completion terms.

Tips and Best Practices:

- **Quick Review of Legal Packs**: In auctions, time is tight. Hire a solicitor experienced in auction purchases to review the legal packs quickly but thoroughly.

- **Avoid Surprises**: Factor in valuation fees and unexpected refurbishment costs before bidding.
- **Act Fast**: Bridging loans are ideal for auction scenarios because they provide quick access to funds—ensure your lender specializes in these types of transactions.

9.2 How to Manage a Refurb Using Bridging

Step-by-Step Guide

1. **Plan Your Refurbishment**
   - Create a detailed plan for the renovation, including timelines, budget, and required permissions. Online tools such as those available on Integer Investments website can help you streamline this process.
   - Obtain multiple quotes from contractors to ensure you get the best price and make sure contractors are reliable and will honor their quotes. To do so, ask for referrals and references.

2. **Set Up the Loan Structure**
   - Choose a rolled-up interest structure if you prefer to avoid monthly payments during the refurbishment phase.
   - Ensure the loan amount (or your cash reserves) includes a buffer for unexpected costs.

3. **Coordinate the Refurbishment**
   - Begin work immediately after completing the purchase.
   - Hold regular meetings with contractors to ensure progress aligns with the timeline.
   - Track expenses meticulously to avoid exceeding your budget.

4. **Monitor Compliance**
   - Ensure all work meets local building regulations and safety standards.
   - Obtain necessary certifications, such as EPCs (energy performance certificate) or HMO licenses, as applicable.

Tips and Best Practices:

- **Budget for Overruns**: Always set aside at least 10 percent of your budget for unexpected costs.

- **Check Contractor Credentials**: Work with insured and experienced contractors to avoid delays or substandard work.
- **Documentation**: Keep all receipts and certifications to streamline your refinance or sale process.

9.3 How to Refinance into a Standard Mortgage

Step-by-Step Guide

1. **Prepare for Refinance**
   - Ensure the property is in good condition (banks do not lend on properties that are not habitable) and ready for valuation. Remember that many banks and valuers have a long process, so consider applying for a new mortgage several weeks in advance.
   - Gather all necessary documents, including proof of income, bank statements, and refurbishment receipts. If needed, improve your credit score, for example by repaying credit cards.
2. **Apply for the Mortgage**
   - Work with a mortgage broker to find a lender offering favourable terms for your property type (e.g., buy-to-let or HMO mortgage).
   - Submit a complete application to avoid delays.
3. **Conduct the Valuation**
   - Arrange for a property valuation through your chosen lender.
   - Ensure the property is clean and well-presented to maximize its appraised value.
4. **Repay the Bridging Loan**
   - Once the mortgage is approved and funds are released, use them to repay the bridging loan in full, including any accrued interest and fees.

Tips and Best Practices:

- **Start Early**: Begin discussions with mortgage lenders or brokers 2 to 3 months before your bridging loan term ends. You might also be able to fix interest rates in advance (you can still lower them, but they won't increase).

- **Maximize Valuation**: Small cosmetic upgrades can increase the property's value, improving your mortgage terms.
- **Exit Fees**: Check whether your bridging loan has exit fees and include them in your financial calculations.

9.4 How to Handle Loan Extensions

Step-by-Step Guide
1. **Identify the Need for an Extension**
   - Recognize early if your project timeline is slipping, such as delays in refurbishment or issues with the exit strategy.
   - Inform your lender as soon as possible to explore extension options and remember that an extension is at their discretion, so you might not obtain it, and you need to look for a new bridge lender.
2. **Negotiate Extension Terms**
   - If possible, discuss the costs involved, including extension fees (typically 3 to 5 percent of the loan amount) and any changes to the interest rate. In many cases, though, these fees are already embedded in your loan and cannot be changed.
   - Consider looking for a new bridge loan as this might be cheaper than extending.
   - Provide a revised timeline and justification for the extension.
3. **Amend the Loan Agreement**
   - Work with your solicitor to finalize the amended terms.
   - Ensure you understand the financial implications, including how additional interest will be calculated.
4. **Adjust Your Exit Strategy**
   - Reassess your exit plan to ensure it aligns with the extended timeline. For example, if refinancing is delayed, begin engaging new lenders immediately.

Tips and Best Practices:
- **Be Proactive**: Communicate with your lender well before the loan term expires to avoid default penalties. Usually bridge

lenders do not like extensions, so make sure you are as transparent and honest as possible.

- **Plan for Extensions**: Include potential extension costs in your initial budget to mitigate financial strain.
- **Exit Strategy Proof**: Strengthen your exit strategy by providing evidence of pending sales or refinancing deals to reassure the lender.

CHAPTER 10

Bridging Finance for Commercial and Mixed-Use Properties

Bridging finance is often associated with residential transactions, such as flips, HMO conversions, or auction purchases. However, **commercial and mixed-use projects** also benefit from short-term funding solutions—whether to secure a rapid purchase, bridge until planning permission is finalized, or refinance an expiring commercial mortgage. This chapter explores how bridging loans are deployed in commercial and mixed-use scenarios, the unique risks involved, and strategies for successful outcomes.

10.1 Understanding Commercial and Mixed-Use Bridging

Defining Commercial and Mixed-Use Properties:

- **Commercial**: Real estate used primarily for business purposes—offices, retail shops, warehouses, hotels, industrial units, and similar assets.
- **Mixed-Use**: A combination of residential and commercial space under one roof—for example, a retail unit on the ground floor with flats above, or an office building partially converted into residential units.

Investors seek bridging finance for these asset classes to meet short-term capital needs—purchasing at a discount, completing refurbishments, or transitioning to a new long-term mortgage. While the overarching concept of bridging is similar to residential deals, **commercial bridging** requires additional valuation, tenant, and yield considerations.

Common Commercial Bridging Scenarios:

1. **Rapid Acquisition for Off-Market Deals**
   - Commercial properties sometimes become available on short notice (e.g., a seller's liquidation). Bridging loans enable fast completion before transitioning to a permanent loan.

2. **Refinancing an Expiring Commercial Mortgage**
   - Borrowers facing a balloon payment or an expiring term can use bridging to buy time for stabilizing the property, securing better tenant agreements, or arranging a more favourable commercial mortgage.

3. **Conversion to Mixed-Use or Residential**
   - Developers might convert unused office floors to residential flats. Bridging covers the initial purchase and refurbishment until the property is suitable for a standard development or commercial mortgage.

4. **Auction Purchases**
   - Much like residential auctions, commercial properties at auction often require completion within 28 days. A bridging loan ensures the short time frames are met when conventional lending is slow or unavailable.

5. **Cash Flow for Large-Scale Upgrades**
   - Investors with multiple commercial units may use bridging to fund capital-intensive improvements (new elevators, re-roofing, retrofitting for regulations) before refinancing onto a lower-rate loan.

10.2 Key Differences from Residential Bridging

Tenant Leases and Valuation:

In commercial and mixed-use bridging, valuers often base their calculations on:

- **Lease Terms:** The stability, length, and strength of tenant covenants are considered. Having a long-term tenant, ideally with a national reputation such as a main street bank, or a supermarket chain, increases the valuation significantly. For example, a property with an outstanding 10-year lease with Tesco can trade at a 5 percent cap, meaning that if Tesco pays £100,000 a year, the value of the property is £100,000/5 percent = £2,000,000. On the other hand, a 3-year lease to a local flower shop might trade at 10 percent. Therefore, even if the flower shop pays the same amount of rent, the same property will be worth half, or £1,000,000, and might even be harder to finance.

- **Rental Income and Yield**: Market rents, yields in the local area, and potential vacancy risk are considered. Higher yields are usually associated with less desirable areas, or higher vacancy risks.
- **Vacant Versus Tenanted**: A building with reliable tenants commands a higher valuation than a partially or fully vacant one. Borrowers with vacant space must provide a leasing plan to reassure the lender of the exit strategy's viability.

LTV and Underwriting Caution:
Commercial bridging lenders commonly adopt **lower LTV caps** (often 60 to 70 percent), especially for specialized assets (e.g., leisure complexes, hotels) or if the area has weaker demand. Some lenders may stretch to 75 percent for prime locations with stable tenants. The underwriting typically scrutinizes:

- Borrower's past experience in commercial real estate
- Strength of existing or prospective tenants
- Realism of the planned exit, such as a future commercial mortgage or a sale to institutional investors

Exit Strategies in Commercial Deals:
Typical exit options include:

1. **Refinancing onto a Commercial Mortgage**: Once occupancy and cash flow are stabilized.
2. **Selling as a Tenanted Investment**: If the building meets the yield expectations of commercial buyers or funds.
3. **Redevelopment**: Converting all or part of the property from commercial to residential. Upon completion or near-future planning

approval, bridging can be refinanced into a specialized development facility or standard mortgage, depending on usage.

10.3 Underwriting Criteria for Commercial Bridging

Detailed Rent Roll and Lease Analysis:
A lender will request existing lease agreements to confirm:

- Remaining lease length and any break clauses
- Rent review terms (e.g., upward-only reviews)
- Strength of tenant covenant (e.g., large corporation versus start-up)
- Compliance with local commercial leasing regulations

Property Condition and Planning:
Commercial bridging often involves:

- **Zoning consents**: If changing from commercial to residential, bridging lenders expect evidence of progress or approvals.
- **Possible partial refurbishment**: Splitting large floors into multiple smaller units or installing essential commercial facilities.

10.4 Case Study: Office-to-Residential Conversion

Scenario: A developer purchases a three-story office block in Manchester to convert the top two floors into six residential flats, retaining the ground floor for office or retail use.

1. **Bridging Loan**: The lender provides £600,000 at 65 percent LTV of the "as is" value (~£925,000).
2. **Refurbishment**: A sum of ~£200,000 is spent on reconfiguring the upper floors. Funds may be released in tranches.
3. **Ground-Floor Tenant**: The developer secures a commercial tenant on a 5-year lease, boosting net operating income.
4. **Refinance**: After ~9 months, stable rent plus newly created residential units raise the valuation to £1.3 million. The developer refinances to a combined commercial/residential mortgage, repaying the bridging loan in full.

10.5 Risks Specific to Commercial and Mixed-Use Bridging

1. **Tenant Default or Vacancy**: Should a major tenant depart, the property's value and liquidity may drop, impairing refinancing or sale prospects.
2. **Longer Marketing Periods**: Commercial properties can take longer to lease or sell, risking extension fees or default interest if bridging extends beyond the original term.
3. **Regulatory Hurdles**: Delays in planning permission or changes in building regulations can stall conversions or expansions.
4. **Economic Cycles**: Commercial assets are more sensitive to market downturns (e.g., retail slumps, oversupply of office space).

10.6 Strategies for Success

1. **Strong Contingency Budgets**: Commercial refurbishments can uncover big-ticket expenses (e.g., roof repairs, HVAC replacements). Reserve at least 10 to 20 percent beyond the planned budget.
2. **Lease Improvement Plans**: For an under-tenanted building, bridging lenders prefer to see a plan for re-leasing or lease renewal. This enhances the exit strategy's credibility.
3. **Professional Valuation**: Commission an independent valuer early to ensure your assumptions about property value and potential rent are realistic.
4. **Clear Exit Timeline**: Commercial refinancing typically needs more lead time than a standard BTL mortgage. Start discussions with commercial lenders well before bridging maturity to sidestep punitive extension fees.

Conclusion: Embracing Commercial and Mixed-Use Bridging

While bridging finance often gets spotlighted in residential contexts, it can be equally transformative in **commercial and mixed-use property** scenarios. Investors use these short-term loans to capitalize on vacant or distressed commercial assets, undertake conversions, or bridge a financing gap while stabilizing tenant occupancy.

Success in commercial bridging hinges on thorough underwriting, realistic timelines, and proactive risk management, especially around tenant leases and local market demand. Coupled with a robust exit strategy—whether a commercial mortgage or a sale to another investor—bridging finance can unlock substantial potential in an ever-evolving commercial real estate sector.

Glossary of Key Bridging Finance Terms

arrangement fee: A fee charged by the lender for setting up a bridging loan. It is typically calculated as a percentage of the loan amount and is usually deducted from the loan advance.

bridging loan term: The duration of the loan, which is usually between 1 and 24 months. The loan must be repaid in full at the end of this term.

closed bridging loan: A bridging loan with a fixed repayment date, often used when there is a clear exit strategy, such as a confirmed sale or refinancing plan.

day 1 drawdown: The portion of the loan amount that is released to the borrower immediately upon completion of the loan agreement. Additional funds may be released later if required for specific purposes, such as refurbishment.

default: When a borrower fails to meet the repayment terms of a bridging loan. Defaults can result in additional charges or enforcement actions by the lender.

development finance: A type of bridging loan used specifically for property development projects, such as new builds or major renovations.

drawdown: The process of transferring the loan funds to the borrower or solicitor. This typically occurs after the lender has completed their checks and approved the loan.

exit fee: A fee payable to the lender when repaying the bridging loan. It is often expressed as a percentage of the loan amount or the total loan balance at the time of repayment.

exit strategy: The planned method for repaying the bridging loan. Common exit strategies include selling the property, refinancing onto a standard mortgage, or using other funds.

first-charge loan: A loan secured by the primary legal charge on a property. This gives the lender priority over other creditors in the event of a default.

gross loan: The total amount of the loan, including any retained interest or arrangement fees.

loan-to-value (LTV): The ratio of the loan amount to the value of the property, expressed as a percentage. For example, if a property is worth £200,000 and the loan is £150,000, the LTV is 75 percent.

net loan: The actual amount of money received by the borrower after all fees and retained interest are deducted.

open bridging loan: A bridging loan without a fixed repayment date. This is often used when the exit strategy is less certain, such as awaiting the sale of a property without a set completion date.

permitted development rights (PDR): A government policy in the UK that allows certain property changes, such as converting commercial properties into residential units, without requiring full planning permission.

refinance: The process of replacing a bridging loan with a longer-term financial product, such as a standard mortgage or buy-to-let mortgage.

regulated bridging loan: A bridging loan that is regulated by the Financial Conduct Authority (FCA) in the UK. These loans are usually secured against a property that is the borrower's primary residence.

retained interest: A method of payment where the interest for the loan term is deducted upfront from the loan amount. This ensures that monthly payments are not required during the term of the loan.

rolled-up interest: Interest that accrues during the loan term and is added to the loan balance, to be paid in full at the end of the term.

second-charge loan: A loan secured by a secondary legal charge on a property. This means the lender is second in line to be repaid, after the first-charge lender.

security: The property or properties used to secure the bridging loan. The lender holds a legal charge on the property until the loan is repaid.

solicitor's fees: The legal costs associated with setting up the bridging loan, including preparing and reviewing loan agreements.

special purpose vehicle (SPV): A limited company set up for the sole purpose of purchasing and holding property. SPVs are often used by investors to optimize tax and finance arrangements.

unregulated bridging loan: A bridging loan that is not regulated by the FCA. These are typically used for business or investment purposes, such as purchasing or renovating an investment property.

valuation fee: A fee paid for the lender to arrange a professional valuation of the property being used as security for the loan.

Index

www.ingramcontent.com/pod-product-compliance
Lightning Source LLC
Chambersburg PA
CBHW061336220326
41599CB00026B/5206